PROPHETIC INTEGRITY

The Dos and Don'ts of PROPHETIC MINISTRY

By Eddie and Alice Smith

WORLD WIDE
PUBLISHING GROUP

7710-T Cherry Park Drive, Suite 224
Houston, Texas 77095

(281) 830-8724

Published in the United States of America

eBook: 978-1-60796-875-7

Softcover: 978-0-692-04796-5

Table of Contents

Chapter One Discovering God's Voice 5

Chapter Two Be Converted 11

Chapter Three Prophetic Knowing 27

Chapter Four Forms of Prophetic Ministry 35

Chapter Five She's a Witch 47

Chapter Six God Still Grants Spiritual Sight 57

Chapter Seven A Supernatural Message Should be
Confirmed by Supernatural Evidence 61

Chapter Eight Spiritual Sensitivity 69

Chapter Nine Solving Prophetic Problems with
Accountability and Integrity 73

Chapter Ten First Person Prophecies 81

Chapter Eleven What about False Prophecies? 87

Chapter Twelve New Testament Prophecy: An Invitation,
or a Declaration? 95

Chapter Thirteen Picking Up the Prophetic Pieces 111

Chapter Fourteen Establish a Communication System 135

Chapter Fifteen Public Prophetic Words 145

"…desire spiritual gifts, but especially that you may prophesy."

1 Corinthians 14:1

Chapter One
Discovering God's Voice

"I will stand my watch and set myself on the rampart, And watch to see what He will say to me..."
(Habakkuk 2:1).

Some years ago Dr. C. Peter Wagner and his wife, Doris invited us to teach at their 120 Sunday School Class retreat. We had been traveling all day. After two flights, a long airport layover, and a two-hour automobile ride through Los Angeles' notorious Friday afternoon rush hour traffic, we walked into the comfortable room that Peter and Doris had reserved for us at a beautiful Desert Palm Springs, California resort. Although we were exhausted, we had only one hour to lay our luggage aside, freshen up, and proceed to the auditorium to begin the service.

I (Eddie) sat down at the piano and led in almost an hour of intimate worship. The 120 Class was an expressive, spiritually hungry group. They were skillful worshippers who were passionate about the Lord. Then Alice stood to teach.

At 10:00 p.m. when she finished I was already dreaming of a warm bath, a change of clothes, and a good night's sleep. It seemed that everyone else was of the same mind...until Peter stood and asked, "How many of you would like to receive personal prophetic ministry from the Smiths' tonight?" One hundred and fifty hands flew up! "Well," he continued, "I'm going to ask the Smiths to minister to you. Come and sit close to the front. As they finish praying with each of you, you may retire to your room."

I was "shell-shocked!"

"Personal prophetic ministry?" I thought, "Me?"

I knew just enough about personal prophecy to realize that I was in big trouble! If you are not familiar with this, what Peter was suggesting was that Alice and I pray over each individual, and share with them what we sensed God was saying to or about them. Although Alice had some experience at this, I had none! What in the world was I going to do?

The past few decades God had put me in several unfamiliar ministry scenarios like this. For me, a Southern Baptist minister, to teach at Charismatic meetings and Pentecostal pastors' conferences around the world has been daunting at times. I learned to ask God for help, and to lean heavily upon Him. He has never left me stranded. Thankfully, He always comes through!

So I asked the Lord what I was to do. His instruction was simple. He spoke to my heart, "Ask each person their name and I'll take care of the rest." Not knowing what was about to happen, by faith I cautiously proceeded.

A young man stepped forward for prayer. "What is your name?" I asked as the Lord had instructed me.

"My name is Peter," the man answered. Immediately I remembered Simon Peter in the Bible and somehow I knew what I was to do.

"Peter," I continued, "Do you feel like everyone else has a testimony for Christ, but you are continually failing to stand for Him?" Peter's head dropped with embarrassment and he tearfully admitted it was true. I ministered to him from the Scripture and prayed as God did a deep work in his heart.

The next person who came forward was a beautiful Asian lady who appeared to be in her mid to late twenties. As the Lord had instructed, I asked her name.

"My name is Ruth," she answered.

Prophetic Integrity

Remembering and applying the biblical story of Ruth, I said, "Ruth, I believe the Lord is telling me that you always feel unworthy to sit at the Lord's table."

Ruth burst into tears. She sobbed deeply saying, "Yes, that's true." She was obviously moved to think that I could know something so deeply personal about her. (1 Corinthians 14:24-25)

"Ruth," I continued, "the Lord wants you to know He delights in calling you His Bride. He does not want you to merely survive, gleaning in the field like a stranger. He wants you to sit at the table with Him in His house. He wants to be your spiritual husband even as you are part of His Bride." I prayed for and ministered God's Word to her.

Then David came. I am sure you get the picture. I said, "David, I feel the Lord is saying that you've committed an awful sin, one that disqualifies you from serving Him in the future. Is this true?"

Sure enough, it was right on target. Thankfully, Alice did most of the personal ministry that night. We dropped into bed sometime after 2:00 a.m. the next morning!

God had graciously compensated for my lack of knowledge and inexperience. And He will be faithful to you as well.

The next morning, Dr. Wagner asked for testimonies from the ministry the night before. Ruth enthusiastically jumped to her feet. Her voice literally danced with excitement as she said, "The night before we left for this weekend retreat I was met with a difficult personal dilemma. The man I have dated the past several years asked me to marry him. My heart was torn. I love and respect him, but I haven't had the peace in my heart to accept his proposal. I agreed that I would answer him when I return. So, I came to the retreat trusting God to tell me if I am to marry him."

"Last night, Brother Eddie ministered a prophetic word to me. What he said was so personal and accurate, that I knew it must be from God. He said that the Lord wants me to eat at His table with Him because I am Jesus' Bride. I know now that I must return and answer 'no.' Jesus is my Bridegroom and I am His Bride. He wants my time and my devotion. I am so happy with my decision."

A couple of times in the ensuing years, we have seen Ruth. On each occasion she has reminded us of that night and thanked us for the revelation she received.

You see, I had no idea the depth of ministry God was performing in this precious woman's heart. I should add that the Lord never again allowed me to use the names of people in the Bible for prophetic ministry. Nor will He allow you. It is not a formula. He is teaching all of us to hear His voice in those times. It never ceases to amaze me how accurate, how appropriate, and how powerful His words are!

Chapter Two
Be Converted

Those in the Church who say that prophetic ministry ended with the completion of the written Word of God are called "cessationists." Something has ceased alright! It's not that God has *ceased speaking* to us; it's that we have in large part *ceased hearing* what God is saying! Why is it that when we say that we're talking to God, it's called prayer; yet when we say He's talking to us, it's called schizophrenia?

Obviously, anyone can carry on a "one-sided conversation" at a grave; but *Jesus isn't dead!* Let's not forget that the same book that warns us against adding anything to Scripture (Revelation 22:18) also says, *"He who has an ear, let him hear what the Spirit says* (present tense) *to the churches"* (Revelation 2:7).

Scripture addresses this problem saying: *"For the heart of this people is waxed gross, and their ears are dull of hearing, and their eyes have they closed; lest they should see with their eyes, and hear with their ears, and understand with their heart, and should be converted, and I should heal them"* (Acts 28:27 KJV). Hey friend, let's open our eyes and ears and allow God to teach us to hear His voice!

Prophetic Integrity

We normally think of conversion as an experience for the lost. Notice Jesus' words concerning Peter. *"But I have prayed for thee, that thy faith fail not: and when thou art <u>converted</u>, strengthen thy brethren"* (Luke 22:32).

What kind of conversion do Christians need? For one, today the Lord is converting many Christians to prayer. People are praying as never before in recent history. But many of us need to be converted from the old, ineffective paradigm of living as deaf servants of a mute God. It's vital that we establish effective two-way communication with Jesus. Remember, a relationship involves two!

Perhaps you heard about the old man whose wife asked him to tell her once more that he loved her.

"My Dear," He said. "I told you I loved you when I married you. If I change my mind, I'll let you know!"

But our favorite joke is the old couple who were almost asleep, when the elderly woman whispered to her husband, "Honey, tell me you love me like you used to."

"I love you," the gruff old man muttered.

"No, honey, tell me you love me like you *used* to," she insisted.

Be Converted

"I love you," the sleepy man said tenderly.

Just as the man was about to doze off, his wife said, "Sweetheart, kiss me like you used to."

Realizing he was not getting sleep otherwise, he leaned over and gave her a reluctant peck on the cheek.

"No, dear, kiss me like you *used* to!"

With that, he planted a generous kiss on her lips, and rolled over to fall asleep.

He'd hardly done so, when she elbowed him and said,

"Darling, nibble on my ear like you used to."

"Do what?" The agitated husband blurted.

"Nibble on my ear like you *used* to!" His doting wife said.

Suddenly, in the darkness, came an awful crashing and banging of items in the room.

"What are you doing, honey?" She asked with alarm.

"Trying to find my teeth…." ☺

Well, the Lord has been telling us of His love and He will never change His mind. Starting in the 1980's God began restoring prophetic ministries in the Church around the world. For years, many evangelicals had lived as though 2,000 years ago, God wrote a best seller, then retired without anything to say since. We've heard it said, "God speaks to Charismatics; He writes to Evangelicals." But no more!

Today's Christians worldwide are listening to the Lord and He is speaking fresh new words; words of comfort, words of confirmation, and words to equip them for spiritual ministry. A new paradigm for many.

Lest you think that intercessory prayer is only talking to God, listen up! The Lord speaks to those who speak to Him!

Growing Accustomed to His Voice

Jesus said, *"My sheep hear my voice"* (John 10:27). Every believer can hear God's voice. However, many have not been taught to hear His voice, and what to do with what they hear. It is also true, we might add, that some believers are especially gifted to do so. In this book, we will address those more specifically.

At times it seems that Alice possesses "spiritual radar." In fact, today I (Eddie) received a call from a pastor who has been a close friend for many years. We recently conducted a conference at his church, when on the first night as Alice was speaking; she stopped abruptly in the middle of her message, turned to the

Pastor and prophesied that within the next six months God was going to open up a major ministry promotion for him.

Now Pastor Chris was calling us with great excitement to announce that God had placed him as senior pastor of a large church in his area of the city.

In Romans 12:6 we are told of the gift of prophecy exercised by some in the Body of Christ. In 1 Corinthians 12:8-10 we see the prophetic gifts outlined. It's been our observation that people with these gifts tend to hear more often and with more clarity than others. As far as the *office* of the prophet goes, few people actually operate in that office partly because the Church at large has not identified and authorized them to do so. (Ephesians 4:11) Pastor John Eckhart is a friend of ours who lives in Chicago, Illinois. He has a church and oversees *The Crusaders Ministries*. John is a master in discipleship and training. This is what he says about the prophetic in his church.

> Our church has a vision to see that believers are released to prophesy. This comes through training and activation. As a result, hundreds of believers have been trained and released to prophesy.

Prophetic Integrity

> Prophetic teams have been formed in the
> church to minister to thousands of
> people regularly. Apostles are graced to
> present new truths such as this, and to
> release the saints to operate in them.[1]

We've mentored intercessors, those whose primary ministry is prayer, for years. We're convinced that a higher than average percentage of them are prophetically gifted. Spending time with Jesus and actively seeking intimacy with Him as they do, they grow accustomed to His voice. Hearing God's voice is natural to their calling. This should not be awkward for us to understand. The Apostle Paul, when describing the Body of Christ in 1 Corinthians 12, refers to the relationships of the various parts of the human body. In verse 16 he writes, *"And if the ear should say, 'Because I am not an eye, I do not belong to the body,' it would not for that reason cease to be part of the body."*

Not too long ago I (Alice) had a dream. It is unusual for me to dream, but this dream was specifically about a nationally known motivational speaker we know. I called him the next day. "James," I said, "Last night I had a dream in which you were considering a purchase of some condominiums that have six or eight units in each section. The fronts are a sandy-colored stucco. I feel the Lord is warning that if you do, it will cause you nothing but trouble. Does this make any sense to you?"

With a response of disbelief, he said, "Yeah, it makes a lot of sense! I just got back from Las Vegas, where four of us agreed to buy the condos you just described. The contract is in the works right this moment. No way am I going to buy them now. Let me get off the phone and stop my part immediately."

About four weeks later, James called to say that the other guys had gone ahead and purchased the condos, and later discovered that the foundations weren't done properly. They were already engaged in a legal battle with the previous owners. James told me, "Alice, you saved me from a potential mess. Thank you so much."

While it's true that all of God's children are to hear Him, those who experience *revelatory gifts* are generally more sensitive to see and hear spiritual realities. Let's call them, as Paul did, the eyes and the ears of the Body of Christ. (1 Corinthians 12:16)

Hey, we Smiths aren't naïve! We clearly understand the debate that exists among Christians concerning the thought of God speaking. One angry pastor pointed to his Bible and warned me (Eddie) stressing, "Brother, everything God has to say is in this book. This is His *complete* revelation. If you claim God speaks to you, you are adding to this book; and *that's extra-biblical!*" Considering the sternness of his reprimand, I was frankly surprised that he called me "brother!" ☺

Adding to the Scripture? No!

"For I testify unto every man that heareth the words of the prophecy of this book. If any man shall add unto these things, God shall add unto him the plagues that are written in this book..." (Revelation 22:18).

Are the prophetic words that God reveals to our hearts tantamount to the Scripture? Absolutely not! Scripture is a *finished* revelation. Although Scripture itself is a finished revelation, God **has not** finished revealing. Is that possible? Sure it is. The fact that you live in a finished home does not necessarily mean that the builder of your home has finished building other homes.

Scripture is not all that God has to say; and John 21:25 tells us that many more about Jesus happened but they couldn't all be added. The Lord continues to speak today. After all, had we not heard His voice, we could never have been born again or called into the ministry. After all, one's "call to the ministry" must be heard. That which is *extra-biblical* is distinctly different from that which is *unbiblical!*

The Extra-biblical VS the Unbiblical

Some are so afraid of being extra-biblical that they have become unbiblical! Case in point, many churches don't allow prophetic ministry because they see it as unbiblical. We would do well to remember how often Scripture admonishes us, *"He that hath an ear,* let him hear *what the Spirit is saying..."* (Revelation 2:7). Remember Jesus' words. *"My sheep* hear my voice..." (John 10:27).

In his book, Confronting *the Powers,* Peter Wagner writes,

> "Jack Deere and Peter Wagner are just two traditional evangelicals and former cessationists [those who believe some spiritual gifts were only for the first century] among rapidly increasing numbers of others who believe that a valid source of divine knowledge comes through what some would call 'extra-biblical revelation.' I dare say that the

standard-brand evangelical doctrine of 'logos only' that we were taught might now find a place on an 'endangered doctrines' list, about to become extinct. As always, I would not fail to reemphasize that any purported extra-biblical revelation that contradicts or violates the written Word of God ipso facto must be rejected by faithful Christians. The Bible remains the only final and authoritative litmus test for divine revelation. The 66 books of the Bible constitute a closed canon."[2]

A pastor friend of ours, having heard me (Eddie) mention that God had spoken to me, accused me of receiving "extra-biblical revelation," therefore practicing the occult!

Ironically, when he receives offerings in his church services he routinely instructs his congregants, "Now, let's bow our heads and close our eyes and ask the Lord how much we should give. As soon as God tells you an amount, then make your check payable to the church and place it in the envelope." Interesting, isn't it, how we interpret God speaking?

Be Converted

Recently this pastor, who does not believe in the spiritual gift "word of knowledge" (who would tell you that the Bible is all God has to say, and accused me of operating in the occult) said, "I've been preparing a message for several weeks. I fully intended to preach it today. But as I entered the auditorium this morning the Holy Spirit told me to put it away. You know I'm not good at extemporaneous speaking, so pray for me."

Obviously, he *does* believe God still speaks! He simply reserves the right to determine which topics God may address. For example, the Lord may tell us who to marry, what college to attend, which sermon to preach, or how much money to place in the offering. But if we claim that God speaks to us about anything else, we are either lying or we are deceived. That is patently ridiculous! Actually, we *should* listen continually for God's voice saying, *"This is the way; walk in it"* (Isaiah 30:21). We love it! Christians everywhere are actually granting our heavenly Father freedom of speech! (Smile, it gets better)

Really, is it any harder for the Lord to reveal to us a secret about someone's past that unlocks the door to their freedom during a time of ministry, than it is for Him to reveal to us which college we should attend? Then why is it so difficult for some to accept that He is capable of revealing either? Both are *words of knowledge*. (1 Corinthians 12:8)

A word of knowledge is a spiritual insight from the Lord that we have no natural way of knowing. Whether God tells us some hidden thing about a person's past, present, or even their future; or how much money we are to place in the offering. They are all *divine revelations*. Are they Scripture, or should we consider them on the same level as Scripture? *Certainly not*. They are extra-biblical; but unless they are contrary to Scripture, they are not unbiblical.

We are friends with well-known evangelists, Morris and Theresa Cerullo. Each of us have preached in their international conferences, schools of prayer, and appeared on their international television broadcasts.

Just the other night we were watching television when Eddie asked me (Alice) if I'd heard from Bro. Morris recently. I told him that I hadn't, but inquired as to why had he asked?

"The Lord has had me pray for him the last couple of days, but today the burden has really intensified," Eddie replied.

I said, "Let's call and pray for him."

When I dialed the number, his wife Theresa answered.

"Theresa, is Bro Morris okay?" I asked. "Eddie has had a burden to pray for him that intensified today."

Theresa said, "I can't believe you are calling, Alice! Yes, Morris needs prayer. We are in the emergency room right now! Morris was taking the trash out (they live on top of a hill) and he fell and rolled down the hill. He is hurting, has a knot on his head and lots of scrapes. *Only God could have had Eddie praying for him at this moment.* Thank you so much."

Theresa handed the phone to Bro. Morris, and we prayed for him. As we ended the call, the Lord reaffirmed Eddie, who had *acted* on the word of knowledge he'd received.

The results? Morris and Theresa were blessed to know their circumstance was on the Lord's heart, and Jesus had someone praying for them in their time of need.

Consider this. Had we not heard from God concerning our sin and the Savior, we could have never been saved. It was more than reading words. We received a revelation in our hearts that we are sinners, and Jesus died for our sin on the cross. As salvation is life changing; a true prophetic word, given at the right time, in the right way, can also be life changing.

God is converting the theology and mindsets of many today. It may move some of us out of our comfort zones, but as the late Pastor John Wimber once pointed out, "God is willing to offend our minds to expose our hearts."

It is possible some Christians who aren't receptive to the idea that God speaks today, haven't argued with the concept as much as with the faulty methods they've seen or stories they've heard.

Isn't it sad that many in the Church are not hearing and speaking what God is saying? The prophets are shut down. The intercessors are cut off. Because of this, some Christians and their neighbors are making the owners of "psychic hotlines" zillionaires! They so want to hear *something* from the spirit world, that they will accept anything regardless of the source. This shouldn't be.

Prophecy at Work

The Hebrew word for "prophet" is *nabi,* derived from a verb signifying "to bubble over like a fountain." [*Strong's Concordance*] The word implies one who announces or proclaims a declaration from God or simply, to speak for another as in the sense a translator repeats the words of the messenger.

A primary role of an intercessor (one whose primary ministry is prayer) is to "plead the cause for another in prayer." So a primary role of a prophet is to "announce a message from God." One speaks *to* God; the other speaks *for* God.

The word "watchman" in Scripture refers to the role of prophet in some verses and to the role of intercessor in others. As an example, in Isaiah 62:6 the watchmen refers to those who are called to pray. Isaiah writes: *"I have posted watchmen on your walls, O Jerusalem; they will never be silent day or night. You who call on the Lord, give yourselves no rest."* However, Hosea 9:8 implies the assignment from God is to act as a prophet. *"The prophet, along with my God, is the watchman over Ephraim, yet snares await him on all his paths, and hostility in the house of his God."* There is a close relationship between prophecy and prayer.

Prophetic intercessors actually prophesy as they pray. In understanding this unique role, our friend Dick Eastman in his book, *The Jericho Hour* says,

"Whenever any sensitive intercessor moves into a prolonged season of intercessory prayer, there is the potential for God to use that person to pray prophetically. Quite often the intercessor will not realize this is happening. If the person does, he or she will recognize that what is being prayed has originated with God. They are, in a sense, praying a 'word' from the Lord."[3]

Chapter Three
Prophetic Knowing

Making matters more complicated, we are told in Numbers 12:8 that although God spoke to Moses face to face, to others (that's us) He speaks in riddles. That is true whether it's through the symbols of one's dream language or in visions like the one Peter experienced on the rooftop at noon. (Acts 10:13-17) Indeed, God speaks to us in mysterious ways.

The Capture of an Evil Dictator

When Iraqi leader, Saddam Hussein, was missing, the U.S. military and allied troops were searching for him. My (Alice's) weekly prayer group received a burden to pray for his capture.

Do you remember the deck of playing cards that the U.S. Government made available? On each card was the photo of one of Sadaam's henchmen. Debbie, one of our ladies, bought a deck for our ladies prayer group to pray through.

We placed them on the coffee table in our prayer room, and began to intercede for God to reveal their hiding places. It took months before the Holy

Spirit began to give us a strategy. We heard the Lord say, "Separate the Full House."

If you are unfamiliar with playing cards, a Full House is when the five cards a person has been dealt, and is holding, includes *three of one suit* (like the Three of Hearts, the Three of Spades, or the Three of Diamonds), plus *two of another suit* (like the Seven of Clubs, and the Seven of Diamonds).

Interestingly, the Full House we saw included five key men from the deck of cards. Saddam, and four of his generals—all from Saddam's hometown of Tikrit. This was important to our revelation. We sensed that these were a strategic stronghold of five. We immediately began to intercede and ask the heavenly Father to confirm this insight.

Within a week one of these important men from what we called "the Full House of Tikrit" was captured. Each week we saw the capture or killing of the evil men that comprised Saddam's murderous regime. Then the week before our Thanksgiving break, we ladies had an amazing spiritual warfare breakthrough.

Eraina saw a vision of a spider hole. Then Kendra saw the words Tigris and Euphrates. Then I felt the number four was significant to the capture of

Saddam Hussein. We felt impressed to count the remaining cards, representing men left to be captured, and there were 13. We asked the Lord to confirm that we were on target by allowing us insight into every key to the puzzle He had given us.

Suddenly, the room felt electrified with the presence of the Lord. We knew we were to continue to fight spiritual darkness, and also agree with the Lord regarding the revelation that we were confident He was unfolding.

Now, allow me to recap.

1. Four of the five key men in the Full House had either been captured or killed. The House was falling.

2. Saddam alone remained missing.

3. We knew a "spider hole" was involved.

4. He would be found at the junction of the Tigris and Euphrates Rivers.

5. The number four was significant to the breakthrough, but we didn't know why.

6. And 13 men were yet to be captured.

At the end of our intercessory meeting that morning we knew the Lord had heard our prayers. We had pinpointed the keys for the capture of an evil dictator who for decades had killed and tortured his people in Iraq. We were confident that we would hear on the news *that day* the good news of his capture. But it didn't happen.

Day two, nothing. Day five, no news. Let me offer a tip at this juncture of the story. God's timing is not ours. The tension we face as prophetic prayer warriors is to stand in faith, not doubt, not manipulate the Word, but celebrate the victory until we see it!

What Happened Next?

The fifth card to collapse the Full House was *Saddam Hussein's*. He was captured by the *4ᵗʰ Infantry* of the U.S. Army on *December 13*, 2003. He was pulled from his hiding place the Army called *a spider hole*, sandwiched between the *Tigris and Euphrates Rivers*. Never underestimate the power of prophetic intercession, along with good accountable teamwork.

Pastors and leaders, for you to disciple your people in this critical area requires that you establish and teach them a system of accountability, and an investment of time and patience.

"Well, you can't let your experience determine your theology." Someone might say. Had we one dollar for every time we've heard that statement, we would be millionaires.

Many years ago our friend Steve Meeks, pastor of Calvary Community Church in Houston, Texas said that he was lamenting to God one day, "Lord, it seems like so many Christians are letting their experiences determine their theology."

When God replied, "Steve, perhaps you've let your lack of experience determine yours."

We've always been blessed to hear Peter Wagner speak when he was anywhere near Houston. Such was the case when Peter addressed several hundred pastors at a Methodist church in Bryan, Texas. However, we were caught off guard that night, at the conclusion of his presentation, when he told the crowd, "now I'm going to ask my friends Eddie and Alice Smith to come minister to you." It was reminiscent of our evening in Desert Palm Springs that we described in Chapter One.

Eddie went to the keyboard where he sat down and began to play extemporaneously. If you aren't accustomed to that, it means he played music prophetically from his heart, rather than songs that were previously written.

I (Alice) moved slowly to the pulpit and waited for direction from the Lord. Slowly and carefully, I spoke directly to several of those pastors, people I didn't know. It sounded something like this.

"May I ask the pastor in the green shirt on the fourth row to stand? Sir, I feel the Lord is telling me that you've been experiencing a real trial in this new church you've recently been called to pastor." With that small amount of information, the pastor was overwhelmed with God's love for him. I continued to share with him what I felt the Lord wanted him to know. It was an encouraging and comforting word. (I never give a humiliating or threatening word in a public forum and rarely give one.)

Fast forward one year. My outgoing brother John, who lived in Waco, Texas walked into the local International House of Pancakes® for breakfast one morning. Glancing around the room, he spotted a gentleman sitting alone with his notepad, pen, and a Bible.

Never a shy person, John walked over to him and said, "Sir, excuse me. Are you a Christian?" A little stunned, the man acknowledged that he was.

Then John said, "I couldn't help but notice your Bible. I am a Christian also. Would you like to have company for breakfast? The stranger pulled the chair out and with a grin said "Sure, sit down."

"Are you reading your daily devotional," John asked?

"No," the man explained. "I'm a pastor. I was re-reading a word that a lady from Houston gave me about a year ago while at a pastor's conference in Bryan, Texas. She said that she felt the Lord tell her 12 things that would occur in my life over the next year. A friend who was with me wrote them down for me. I just checked off the last item. Everything the lady shared that night has come to pass in the past 12 months. Amazing!"

"Was her name Alice Smith?" John asked.

Obviously shocked, the pastor answered, "Why yes, that was her name! How did you know that?"

"Alice is my sister," John explained. What he *didn't* mention was that I and 3,000,000 other people live in Houston!

We've asked ourselves why Jesus put those two men at that table on that day, at an IHOP in Waco, Texas. Perhaps it was to acknowledge, encourage, and confirm to me that I had heard Him correctly on that night, a year earlier, in Bryan, Texas. Then again, perhaps it was to encourage my brother John to be a bold witness. It could also have been God's way of confirming the prophetic word the pastor had held to for an entire year.

It's difficult to find anyone who does not believe we are living in the last days. Revival is stirring in war torn Africa, parts of the Middle East, South America and China's conversion rate is exploding. We are seeing the beginnings of Joel 2:28, *"And afterward, I will pour out my Spirit on all people. Your sons and daughters will prophesy, your old men will dream dreams, your young men will see visions."* From the perspective of this prophetic word, words of knowledge, interpretation of dreams and visions will increase, not decrease! Make sure you are on board.

Chapter Four
Forms of Prophetic Ministry

- It seems clear from Scripture that prophecy will take a more central place in the end-time church. Let's consider a few key thoughts. Prophetic or revelatory ministry takes various forms. God speaks to us today through various means.
- He speaks to us through His written Word.
- He speaks to us through godly counsel.
- He speaks to us when we pray. Again, prayer is a dialogue, not a monologue.
- He speaks to us through dreams and visions. Amazingly, some protest the idea that God speaks to people through visions, but have no problem believing that God could speak to them through dreams. That is to say, if you claim to hear from God while you are awake, and not asleep, we should be suspicious. Silly, isn't it?
- He speaks to us through pastors, teachers, and evangelists.

- He speaks to us through a team of prophets. (People with prophetic gifts.)

- He speaks to us through impressions or deep spiritual knowing; through our inner self, our spirit man.

- He speaks to us through the spiritual gifts of prophecy. These prophetic gifts include words of knowledge, words of wisdom, and discerning spirits.

Our Need for Discernment

According to Scripture, the Lord *sees and hears* certain things, which directly implies that He chooses *not to see and hear* others. For instance, Psalm 34:15-17 says,

"The eyes of the Lord are on the righteous and his ears are attentive to their cry; the Face of the Lord is against those who do evil, to cut off the memory of them from the earth. The righteous cry out, and the Lord hears them; he delivers them from all their troubles."

Since God sees and hears the righteous when they pray, we can trust Him to intervene when we receive a destructive prophetic word. Do we assume the Lord wants to come in judgment? No. We believe that God desires to deal mercifully with us. James 2:13 says, *"Mercy triumphs over judgment;"* and Isaiah 55:7 says, *"Let the wicked forsake his way and the evil man his thoughts. Let him turn to the Lord, and he will have mercy on him, and to our God, for he will freely pardon."*

Sadly, some receive negative prophetic words as declarations of doom, rather than invitations to intercede for victory. This is illustrated in the Book of Amos. Amos was a simple shepherd with a big heart who spoke against social evils and materialistic lifestyles in his day. Amos' name literally means "to bear a load."

Written in the eighth century B.C, Amos was burdened with the sin of the northern kingdom of Israel. For six chapters Amos changes roles. In Chapter 7 he writes; *"This is what the Sovereign LORD showed me; He was preparing swarms of locusts after the king's share had been harvested and just as the second crop was coming up. When they had stripped the land clean, I cried out, 'Sovereign Lord, forgive! How can Jacob survive? He is so small!' So the Lord relented. 'This will not happen,' the Lord said"* (Amos 7:1-3).

Next, the Lord revealed to Amos a great fire that He had prepared to punish them. The fire burned up the waters and was about to devour the land. Amos interceded in verse five, *"Sovereign Lord, I beg you to stop..."*

> *"So the LORD relented. 'This will not happen either,' the Sovereign LORD said.*
>
> *Then he showed me this; The Lord was standing beside a wall built with a plumbline, checking it with a plumbline to see if it was straight. And the Lord said to me, 'Amos, what do you see?' I answered, 'A plumbline. Then God said, 'I will test my people with a plumbline. I will no longer turn away from punishing'"* (Amos 7:6-8).

At this point Amos did not pray. He didn't cry out for mercy. Why not? Did destruction follow because Amos didn't at least pursue an intercessory breakthrough? We will never know until we reach heaven, but it's a good lesson for us. In such a case, it's wise for us to take the issue to prayer, and pray until we sense a breakthrough, or a warning in our hearts that we are to stop praying.

The inevitable consequences that threatened the people should have energized Amos to "stand in the gap again." In Amos 3:7 we read, *"Surely the Sovereign Lord does nothing without revealing His plan to His servants the prophets."* Sin requires judgment. Historically, whenever God has found someone who would intercede for sinners, He has shown himself merciful.

Receiving Prophetic Revelation

How do we receive a prophetic word from the Lord? In *The Elijah Task* the late John Sandford states,

*"Numbers 12:1-8 lists five ways God speaks to men. The most indirect way, which involves the least interference from the conscious mind, is through a **dream.***

The second is by **vision.** There are three types of visions: a **trance,** in which the mind is nearly totally arrested; or a **picture** flashed upon our inner screen while we are vividly alert; or a **direct seeing** into the world of the spirit.

The third way is called '**dark speech."** In dark speech God uses language figuratively. Language comes into the mind; the mind is involved, but the message itself is something beyond present comprehension. The mind is used but still bypassed.

The fourth step up the ladder is **direct speech.** We still hear this within our spirits, but God is speaking clearly to our minds. There are no puns, no parables, 'Get up and go to church' means that you should get up and go to church.

Finally, the fifth way is the most clear; He **speaks audibly**, as Aaron, Miriam, and Moses all heard Him…"[4]

Once you sense the Lord has given you prophetic insight, ask the Holy Spirit for further illumination. There is a big difference between faith and presumption. Presumption is an opinion based on an assumption. Faith is a commitment based on known truth. Faith is never a leap in the dark, it's always a step in the light.

Let's always maintain teachable spirits. No one likes to be around a "know it all" who stalks around like an undisciplined, impatient "Rambo." The Bible instructs us in 1 Peter 5:8, *"Be self-controlled and alert. Your enemy the devil prowls around like a roaring lion looking for someone to devour!"* If we fail to demonstrate godly accountability, WE may be the ones being devoured!

Intercessors who hear and obey God will at times be criticized for following what may appear to some to be illogical and unreasonable. Following prophetic assignments requires both faith and perseverance. There will occasionally be some who'll want to control you. Some will accuse you of missing great opportunities, missing God and even misinterpreting prophecy. Walk humbly and serve patiently. After all, to boldly march around Jericho seven times; to confidently collect five small stones to confront a nine-foot giant; to dutifully bathe your leprous body in a muddy river; and to obediently step into a blazing furnace were anything but sensible!

Discerning Spirits

The gift of discerning spirits, mentioned in 1 Corinthians 12:10, is the spiritual ability God gives some to judge and to distinguish between spirits. It is an intuitive, spiritual knowing. Early in our marriage, I (Eddie) was frankly uncomfortable with some of Alice's comments because I misunderstood her. Since I don't have the gift of discerning spirits I thought she was merely guessing; or worse yet, just being critical.

The truth, is I judged her based on my lack of spiritual understanding. But many years have passed and now I see how the Lord has used Alice's prophetic words to bless thousands around the world.

We drove into the parking lot of a wonderful church in the Dallas, Texas area one sunny day. I (Eddie) climbed out of the motor home in which we lived, and went into the church office to meet the pastor. Unfortunately, he was out to lunch, and I was told that he would return in one hour.

As I left to return to the motor home, I noticed a stack of free church photo directories on a table. Back in the 1970s, virtually every church produced directories with family photos and contact information of their members. I thought it might help me to become familiar with the names and photos of their leadership team.

When I stepped back inside the motor home, Alice asked about it. I showed it to her and she took it to the back for a time of prayer.

After 30-45 minutes she brought the directory back to me saying, "Honey, as I prayed over each family I sensed the Lord was giving me insight into what might be going on in the lives of some of them. I wrote that beside their photos."

Sure enough, she had written notes like "unsaved," "needs healing," "marital discord," and such. I asked her if I could show her notes to the pastor I was about to meet. She was reluctant, saying "But I don't know if what I've written is correct." I assured her that he would understand the risk she took.

I took the book with me when I returned to meet the pastor. During our conversation, I showed him what she had written. Tears came to his eyes and he said, "Who told her these things?" I explained that she felt the Lord showed them to her as she prayed over the families. He said, "She knows none of them. I know all of them. What she has written seems quite accurate to me."

That began a wonderful friendship with that pastor that we enjoyed for more than 30 years until he went to be with the Lord.

I (Alice) suggest that the Lord monitors our discernment and decisions to determine when we are ready for promotion. To sow discord, gossip, or to unjustly judge others is proof that we aren't ready to move into the next level of authority.

Some who have the gift of discerning spirits are judgmental. Walking in the flesh, they experience the gift, but fail to exercise the godly discipline that should accompany the gift. Rather than intercede, which is the reason God gives them revelation, they become negative and critical. Thoughtlessly they gossip the revelation with which they have been entrusted. Carelessly, they inadvertently spread rumor and sow discord.

God shares His heart with us so we can bear the burdens of others before the throne, not so we expose the burdens of others before the people! To be able to hear Him with any clarity is a gift. However, this gift also carries a great responsibility. *"From everyone who has been given much, much will be demanded"* (Luke 12:48).

A Christian with this gift often sees the spiritual dimension. This is particularly important because the spirit world *is* the real world. Before anything physical existed, God was! The spirit realm preceded the sense world, and it will continue long after this physical world dissolves. So in one sense, the spirit world is the substance, the physical world is the shadow. (2 Corinthians 4:18; 2 Corinthians 5:7, 16)

Some who experience the gift of discerning spirits can uniquely discern manifestations of the Spirit of God. Perhaps it's due to human nature. However, we've noticed that when many people think of the ability to discern spirits they focus on discerning evil spirits.

While that is often the case, as revival manifestations increase, it will be increasingly important that we are able to identify the work of the Holy Spirit, and to distinguish it from a work of the enemy.

When I (Eddie) was a worship leader in the 1980s, my heart was to lead our congregation into the presence of the Lord to encounter Him. True worship is both an expression and an experience. There were times when our congregational encounter with the Holy Spirit was unmistakable. His presence was virtually palpable. They were holy moments when it seemed as if time was suspended.

I've never seen myself as one particularly gifted to discern spirits, including the Holy Spirit. For that reason, I knew several spiritually mature members of our church, who were blessed with the gift of discerning of spirits. Many times, when I felt we were beginning to encounter the Holy Spirit during our worship times I would keep my eye on them. I could almost read by their expressions what the Lord was wanting to do.

This gift also enables a person to test the spirits of men. Christians with discernment can often distinguish between sincerity and falsehood. (1 Corinthians 2:15) I (Alice) experience this gift at times. There have been occasions in our marriage, after we have heard a salesperson's pitch, that I have already discerned the salesperson's spirit. Is he telling us the truth? Does he have ulterior motives? A person who discerns spirits will often sense the hidden agendas of others. It is not intellectual; it is intuitive. The Lord tells them. Misused, this gift can make one suspicious, cynical, or judgmental, which is why all of the spiritual gifts, Paul said, are to be governed by love.

Spiritual leaders would be wise to determine who of their members are gifted in this regard. Those people might be good to place on certain committees; or as "silent partners" to tag along with them as they meet with bank officers, attorneys, politicians or others with whom the ministry is to do business.

This gift equips some to discern the demonic and angelic worlds. People with the gift of discerning of spirits can be quite helpful in the ministry of deliverance. They often correctly identify the individual demonic spirits with which the ministry team is dealing. During our almost 42 years in facilitating deliverance, the Lord has often revealed to one or both of us the number, and even the names of the demonic spirits residing in a victim to whom we are ministering. Of course, this can be quite disconcerting to the demons since they typically prefer to remain hidden. However, God gives us the victory!

Chapter Five
She's a Witch

The weeklong revival began on Monday night at the First Baptist Church in a small town in the Texas Panhandle. Nearing the conclusion of the first service Alice pointed out a teenage girl seated near the back of the auditorium.

"She's a witch," she whispered.

We agreed to pray all week for the girl. At the close of the last night of the revival I (Eddie) walked to the pulpit to express our thanks to the church when the Spirit of God fell on me. Some people call it *the anointing*; others call it *the mantle* of the Holy Spirit. Whatever, it was God! The empowerment felt as if I was charged with a million volts of heavenly electricity! Terrified that I would say or do the wrong thing and grieve the Holy Spirit, I told the pastor what I sensed and asked him what I should do.

"Obey God," he said wisely.

For several minutes I stood at the pulpit waiting silently for the Lord's instruction as the curious, but expectant congregation stared at me.

Finally, I nervously said, "I feel the Lord is saying that it's time for us to repent. Each of us should obey God."

The spiritual atmosphere was electric with expectancy. A holy hush filled the air, and then minutes later, people all over the auditorium began to weep and confess their sins aloud to the Lord, and to each other.

Suddenly, without warning, the teenage girl that Alice had mentioned earlier in the week leapt to her feet and screamed at the top of her lungs, *"Somebody help me, I'm a witch!"*

Those country folks gasped in disbelief. The atmosphere grew tense. I motioned for the evangelist and Alice to lead the girl into the pastor's study where they ministered to her. During that time, I carefully explained to the shaken congregation what God was doing and led them in fervent prayer for the young woman's salvation and deliverance.

Brokenness and repentance continued in the auditorium. Thirty minutes later, the door opened, and the three of them returned. Peaceful tears bathed the girl's transformed face. She'd been delivered of several evil spirits, which opened the way for her to receive Christ as her Lord and Savior. As she stood to testify to the congregation, she explained how her parents had moved the family from Boston, Massachusetts to Texas. In the family's practice of witchcraft and shamanism, they had been forced to leave the state for counseling without a license. Little did her parents know that their daughter, by a divine plan known only to God, had come to Texas so the Lord Jesus could save and set her free.

On that Monday night service the Holy Spirit had confirmed by Alice's prophetic word that the girl was a witch. Some, as we've said, call this a "word of knowledge," or the ability to know without natural knowledge. Others might say it was "discerning spirits," in this case the spirit of witchcraft. (1 Corinthians 12:8, 10) Perhaps it was both. Our job in this case wasn't to announce the revelation, but to intercede. As Alice often says, "God reveals to heal." Prayer cover almost always precedes the exposure of the demonic.

Listen, you don't have to be an intercessor to have spiritual discernment. Yet, some of the manifestation gifts *tend* to show up in the lives of prophetically gifted praying people more often as tools for the tasks and assignments given them.

We live in a day when spiritual discernment is critical. The enemy has worked rather quietly behind the scenes until recently. We are familiar with the assault of the devil toward God in Isaiah 14, as he boasts, *"I will be like the Most High."* But four chapters earlier, in Isaiah 10:13-14, he declares:

"For he saith, By the strength of my hand I have done it, and by my wisdom; for I am prudent: and I have removed the bounds of the people, and have robbed their treasures, and I have put down the inhabitants like a valiant man: And my hand hath found as a nest the riches of the people: and as one gathereth eggs that are left, have I gathered all the earth; and there was none that moved the wing, or opened the mouth, or peeped."

Far too long the Church has ignored Satan's robbing nations of their treasures and illegally taking territory that isn't his. The real indictment is the latter part of this passage. *"...there was none that moved the wing, or opened the mouth, or peeped."* Aren't we glad that the prophetic spiritual gifts are being activated and that more and more Christians today *are* "flapping their wings," opening their mouths and demanding that the enemy shut up and get out? Today, prayer teams continually travel to pray on site with insight at strategic trouble spots around the world. Right now, I (Alice) am on a plane, on my way to do this very thing.

Evil is coming out of the closet more and more. With the increase of ISIS, Muslim Brotherhood, Hamas, Al-Qaeda, the Taliban, and all the new versions of terrorist organizations that are anxious to shed innocent blood, we should be increasingly discerning. Scripture teaches us that the "shedding of innocent blood defiles the land." Let's look at some of these passages.

- Numbers 35:33, "*So you shall not defile the land in which you are. For blood defiles the land. And the land cannot be cleansed of the blood that is shed in it, except by the blood of him that shed it.*"

- Psalm 106:38, "*...and shed innocent blood, even the blood of their sons and of their daughters, whom they sacrificed to the idols of Canaan; and the land was defiled with blood.*"

- Ezekiel 22:4, "*You are guilty in your blood that you have shed; and you have defiled yourself in your idols you have made. And your days are brought near, and have come to your years. Therefore, I have made you a reproach to the nations, and a mocking to all lands.*"

- Ezekiel. 36:18, *"So I poured My fury on them, because of the blood that they had shed on the land, and for their idols by which they defiled it."*

- Amos 1:13 *Thus saith the LORD; For three transgressions of the children of Ammon, and for four, I will not turn away the punishment thereof; because they have ripped up the women with child of Gilead, that they might enlarge their border:*

This kind of evil was prophesied concerning the end times. Not all pastors have the gift of discerning spirits. Some should, as the Old Testament kings often did, rely on those who do. An old-time preacher was preaching about spiritual discernment.

"He said, 'Go out and look at the stars. You can see or hear nothing worthy of note. You satisfy yourself that there is nothing unusual. Then go into the house and tune in on your long-distance receiving set (radio). At once you hear sounds, you get a snatch of a song, a

word of a speech, a few notes from a
piano, or the solemn tones of an organ.
There is something uncanny about it.
You realize that the air is filled with
sounds the unaided senses know nothing
of. When you look up at the sky again,
you ask what else is there about us of
which we are unaware.

I am not speaking this in order
that I might tell of radio, but in order that
I may illustrate from this branch of
human knowledge the things to which
the Bible has ever borne witness. The
new knowledge illuminates our old
beliefs. The Bible tells us of a higher
sphere and of the existence of things that
cannot be seen or heard with the
ordinary senses. Spiritual things are
spiritually discerned.'"[5]

The Lord is teaching His Church how to operate
as a body. No longer can the ministry be a performance
by professional ministers. It's time for a collaboration
of the gifts within the Body of Christ. Leaders should
develop their own prophetic gifts and abilities.
"Turfism" must give way to "teamwork." Some

should boldly move out of the adolescent spirit, grow to spiritual adulthood, and abandon jealousy and control.

Beyond that, today's leaders should identify and partner with those who have revelatory gifts, and spiritual discernment, just as they would those who are mercy-showers, administrators, or givers. The mature operation and expression of spiritual gifts are crucial if Christ's Kingdom is to advance! However, here is a word of caution.

"Beloved, believe not every spirit, but try the spirits whether they are of God: because many false prophets are gone out into the world" (1 John 4:1).

One day a lady called my office to instruct me (Eddie). Although a total stranger to me, she said authoritatively,

"Brother Smith, the Lord would say unto thee today, 'My son, I have seen your...'"

"Wait a minute," I interrupted gently. "Who are you?"

"I am a prophetess of the Lord," she answered proudly.

"And who says you are a prophetess of the Lord?" I asked patiently.

"Why, I do," she snapped indignantly.

"Who is your pastor and what does he say about your gifts?" I further inquired.

Hotly she replied, "Sir, my pastor doesn't understand my gifts..."

I sighed, "Neither do I lady, neither do I. Have a nice day."

The prophetic gift is valid. But friends, there are some real "fruitcakes" out there in the Church at large! Be careful to whom you submit yourself for spiritual guidance. There is too much at stake! True prophetic people do not gloat in their gifts, but humbly restrain themselves and submit to the leadership and authority of the Holy Spirit.

Prophetic Integrity

Chapter Six
God Still Grants
Spiritual Sight

As difficult as it may be for some of us to accept, many rational, well-balanced Christians routinely see spiritual entities such as angels and demons. Of course, the Bible is full of examples of people who encountered spiritual beings. Unfortunately, many today discount and some deny their God-given gift of spiritual sight. Why is that?

First, in many cases, it's because they are afraid of what they see. They have little or no appreciation for their gift because they have not been taught the value of their gift, and how it's to be effectively used in ministry.

Second, some are reluctant to accept their gift because; they've been misunderstood by others. They see things in the spirit realm, yet are reluctant to admit it to others for fear of being judged or rejected. When we mention this in public teaching, people often approach us privately to express gratitude for our acceptance and affirmation of them, and their experiences. Many of these spiritual warriors have never found anyone with whom they could share this phenomenon. Bottom line? God has uniquely equipped some of us with spiritual sight.

A Christian psychologist called one day to question my (Eddie) judgment. "Rev. Smith," she said, "one of my patients recently came to you for ministry and you told her she's not hallucinogenic."

"That's right...."

"But sir, she sees things that aren't there."

I said, "she sees things..."

The psychologist interrupted, "She sees things that *are there*?"

The spirit realm is weird! If you don't think so, just read your Bible. Every time anyone saw or encountered spiritual entities, it was strange. Angels typically appeared saying two words, "Fear not." This experience can be frightening! Yet spiritual sight and hearing are gifts God initiates. These revelatory abilities are His gifts to the Church. Spiritual sight and hearing are necessary tools to do the spiritual work of God. Let's identify, affirm, and instruct those who have them. If we provide them with a workable system of accountability, and guidelines on how to submit to leadership, these valuable gifted people will feel safe to risk sharing at the proper time, in the proper way, what they sense the Lord may be saying or doing. Most importantly, let's not allow what God has meant to be *a call*, be wrongly diagnosed as *a curse*!

The argument that prophets were only for Old Testament times, and the first century church is biased thinking. If pastors, teachers, evangelists are still needed, then why not the prophet, and the apostle? The Word of God is not like a buffet dinner where we take what we want and leave what we don't want. Nor is it like the fast food giant *Burger King* where "we have it our way!" Until the Church reaches *"unity in the faith"* and attains to *"the whole measure of the fulness of Christ,"* we should honor the ministry of true prophets and apostles along with pastors, teachers, and evangelists! (Ephesians 4:11-13)

Prophetic Integrity

Chapter Seven

A Supernatural Message Should be Confirmed by Supernatural Evidence

Western society denies what the rest of the world knows. We are living in the midst of two simultaneous realities! Some describe us Westerners as "people of the excluded middle," who tend to believe in the third heaven where God is (2 Corinthians 12:2), and the first heaven which we see. But we know little about the second heaven, which is the current realm of Satan, the prince of the power of the air. (Ephesians 2:2)

Those in the third world developing nations live with the daily reality of the spirit world. They often see, experience, and recognize demonic activity. When we come with the Gospel of Christ, they have every right to expect our supernatural message to be confirmed by supernatural evidence. (1 Corinthians 4:20)

You may disagree, but we have reason to believe that babies are born seeing spiritual realities (angels, demons, and other spiritual beings). In our ignorance, many parents teach them not to. Children who complain about a monster in their room may not be imagining anything. They may see what is really there; things beyond their ability to describe. When well-intentioned parents walk into the room and turn on the lights to prove that nothing is there, it may be the parent and not the child who needs instruction!

Rather than attempt to explain away what our children saw, we sought to help our children make sense of what they were seeing, and taught them how to best process it. We did this by asking questions rather than giving instruction or reacting in fear.

Such an encounter might sound like this:

Parent: "What did you see?"

Child: "I don't know."

Parent: "Do you feel it's something good or something bad?"

Child: "Good."

Parent: "Wonderful, do you think it is one of God's angels?"

Child: "Yes."

Parent: "Great! Let's pray and thank Jesus for putting His angel in your room to watch over you."

On the other hand, we might ask:

Parent: "Is it good or bad?"

Child: "Bad."

Parent: "O.K., no problem. Isn't it great to know that Jesus is greater than those bad things? Ask Jesus to make it go away."

Child: "Jesus, make this bad thing go away."

Parent: "Now look. Where is it?"

Child: "Gone."

Parent: "Good. See how much God loves you? See how He answers you when you pray? I love you sweetheart. Now go to sleep. Jesus is here to watch over you."

Through the years, we taught our children not to fear, but rather how to interact with the Lord concerning fearful issues. Spiritual sight is meant to be a blessing, not a burden.

I (Alice) was around seven years old when I first experienced a frightening encounter with a demon. Our family was playing board games together when, for some reason, I needed to go to my room. As I turned the light on in my room, I saw a demon that was black, similar to the size of a cat. Its eyes were red and skin like shiny black vinyl with scales. This demon growled at me and suddenly it streaked across my room and disappeared. I was frozen with fear for a moment, and then ran as fast as I could out of the room to my mother.

I told mother what I had seen. We were a strong evangelical Southern Baptist family, who hadn't been instructed or received any revelation concerning such things. NOTE: *Each of us responds according to the revelation we've received.*

Mother sweetly said, "Oh, Alice Lee that is of the devil. Don't do that!" I thought.... *Don't do what?* I didn't invite that demon into my room. Obviously, I didn't want to be of the devil so I shut spiritual sight off until in college a professor explained how God could use my gift of discernment if I was prayerful. We will talk more about proper use of spiritual gifts later in this book.

With our children, we made sure they felt comfortable talking with us about their supernatural experiences. We could tell you many stories about their encounters. We'll share one.

We had just completed our annual Christmas visit to my (Eddie's) parent's house. We had enjoyed our visit. Dad was president of an English second language Christian high school on the Texas/Mexico border. He had been called out of retirement to that position, after serving the Lord more than 50 years as a denominational worker, pastor, seminary professor, and missionary.

Mother did what women of her generation always did at the end of family visits. She collected all the leftovers and carefully prepared them for us to eat along the way. In her day, there were no fast-food roadside restaurants on every corner.

Then we gathered in a circle at the front door, and took hands for a parting prayer.

Our two youngest children, Bryan and Ashlee, were with us. Bryan was 15 years and Ashlee was five years old. As the prayer ended, I asked them if they saw anything in the room. They knew I was referring to anything in the spiritual dimension. Ashlee saw nothing. Bryan, always humble, saw something. He nodded slightly, "yes."

"What do you see, son?"

"I see a sign," he replied.

"A sign? What kind of sign?" I asked.

"It's a white sign with red letters above the couch," which was in the center of the room.

"What does the sign say?"

"I don't know," he said. "It's not in English. It's written in some sort of characters like Japanese or Korean."

NOTE: *We've learned through the years that spiritual things cannot always be processed by our natural minds.* So, I asked...

"What do you feel the message is?"

"It's a warning," he explained.

"Who is warning who?" I asked.

"God is warning the enemy... oh, I know." He struggled to make sense of it. "It's like when a dog wets on a tree, Dad."

"As I understand it, Son, that's to declare ownership."

"I know what it says, now. It says, 'This far and no further.' God is warning the enemy to stay away from granddaddy and grandmother."

I said, "It reminds me of Song of Solomon 2:4, 'His banner over me is love.' Well, let's go." I turned to leave.

"Dad," Bryan interrupted. "That's not all."

"What else?"

"The letters on the sign…" He teared up a bit. "The letters on the sign are *alive.*"

"Bryan, do you mean like 'living words' of God?"

He nodded, "yes."

On the way home, we discussed what he'd seen. We came to the conclusion that just as an audio recording device can record our spoken words, which can be reheard later; when God speaks, His spoken words must linger forever."

Chapter Eight
Spiritual Sensitivity

We have long-time precious friends in whose home a demon often appeared to their young children as a huge, smoky, brown ghost. The children no longer feared the apparition. They had frankly grown accustomed to its presence. Ugh! However, the parents couldn't understand why, after much prayer, the evil spirit wouldn't leave.

Later, through the help of a team of prophetically gifted Christians who prayed through the house, we discovered that the spirit was related to a Native-American painting in their living room, painted by a shaman (or witch doctor). In fact, posted on the back of the painting was a sticker that explained it was the shaman's practice to assign a spirit to each of his completed paintings. With this revelation, the parents destroyed the expensive painting, and we led them to announce to the demonic entity associated with it that it had no legal right to remain and must leave. With the painting destroyed and the demon evicted, the children never saw the "ghost" (demon) again, hallelujah! *NOTE: Not all Native American artwork is demonic. Some of it however, as it is in other parts of the world, is based on spirit beings and spirit worship;*

unlike our western culture, where art is typically based on realism. One must use caution.

There is no place on Earth where we will no longer encounter the demonic realm. If there were such a place, it would likely be the place of prayer or the study of Scripture. We know, however, satanic forces will assault both of these sacred places at times. The world in which we live is a filthy, fallen battlefield. The reality is, we will contend with spiritual darkness until Christ returns and disposes of it. God never promised anyone a "demon-free zone" in which to live. Jesus encountered them routinely, and from time to time, so will we. In fact, Jesus' first public encounter with a demon was in the synagogue. (Luke 4:33) But rejoice! God promised that He'd prepare a table before us *in the presence* of our enemies! (Psalms 23:5) So let them watch you "eat, drink and be merry" in the presence of your King and Father, Jehovah!

However, note that there is a big difference between an occasional *visitation* by a demonic spirit and their continual *habitation*. Though demons will occasionally drift, or be sent into our homes; we want our lives and homes so cleansed, so that a demonic habitation will cost the enemy more than it will cost us! We deal with these things in our best-selling book,

Spiritual House Cleaning. (Available at www.PrayerBookstore.com)

Spiritual sensitivity seems to be quite common to intercessors. Wisely, they rarely talk about what they sense spiritually. Perhaps it's just as well. Many logical, rational Americans would neither understand nor believe them. I (Eddie) predict that in the days to come, as wickedness worsens, and revival is poured out upon the earth, the Church will look for those who are *the* eyes and *ears* in the Body.

"God is a Spirit," Jesus says in John 4:24. The more spiritually sensitive we are, the more prepared we are to commune with Him. However, spiritual sensitivity can also present a problem. Because the spirit-world is a reality beyond the sense-world, spiritually sensitive people tend to be sensitive to *everything* spiritual. At times, they receive revelation from both the second heaven (the demonic realm) and the third heaven (the Throne of God). Differentiating between the voice of the enemy, the voice of God, and their own inner voice can be difficult, especially in the beginning.

For that reason, spiritually sensitive Christians should take precaution against deception by walking in accountability with those more seasoned in spiritual things. True, God has more power to protect us than the enemy has to deceive us. Yet, we also have personal responsibilities related to our protection. For one, heaven-sent spiritual insights or revelations will never contradict the Word of God.

Chapter Nine
Solving Prophetic Problems with Accountability and Integrity

It was fall, and the leaves were turning. I (Eddie) was teaching at a prayer conference in beautiful upstate New York, when a charming Charismatic pastor and his wife lamented the recent devastation of their church family.

"It happened in only a matter of weeks," they confided.

One Sunday morning "a prophetess" visiting their church stood and spoke a prophetic word (in the first person) over their congregation. NOTE: *If you are unfamiliar with this kind of prophecy, the lady spoke in the first person, for God; as if God was speaking.*

The pastor described it like this. *"Thus saith the Lord. I, the Lord God, love thee, my people. Because you love Me, and art a blessing to My heart, I have sent to thee My daughter ...* (referring, of course, to herself) *... who will guide you to My perfect will."*

Notice the setup. *"Thus saith the Lord. I, the Lord God, love thee, my people."* Who would doubt the next statement? *"I have sent to thee My daughter, who will guide you to My perfect will."* Who would doubt it? *A discerning person would,* that's who*!* After all, we are instructed to "judge all things" (1 Corinthians 2:15). It was nothing more than a demon-inspired prophetic setup to dismantle the pastor's relationship with his people.

Within days this lady was meeting privately with members of the church. She was filling their heads with nonsense. She drove a wedge between the people and their pastor and his wife (who were God's ordained leaders). Within weeks, the deceived woman was gone, the church was in shambles, the members were scattered and confused, and the hearts of the pastor and his wife were broken. This couple, whose church had been decimated, were shocked to hear my counsel.

As an example, I pointed across the room to a man who was the featured soloist for the conference we were attending. I asked, "Do you know anything about Bro. Jones (not the singer's real name)?"

"No, I don't," the pastor answered.

"Well," I continued. "Would you be willing to invite him right now to come sing at your church?"

"Sure," he replied enthusiastically. "He has a wonderful singing voice."

Then I explained. "Before I would invite him, or anyone else to minister in my church, I would want to know who they are and where they're from. I would like to talk with their pastor about their character, and the level of credibility they have in their local church." The pastor looked at me shocked, shaking his head in recognition of what he had just learned.

Responsible pastors are careful about who they allow to step into their pulpits. However, in our travels we've met ministers who float in and out of churches without either personal or ministry accountability. They bank on the fact that enough pastors are too busy or too gullible to check them out. In these final days of history, it is even more critical than in the past to check references for everyone from nursery workers, members of our worship teams, and certainly those who fill our pulpits.

One minister we know was in the process of divorcing his third wife on grounds of "incompatibility" when he came to me for counsel. I (Eddie) mentioned the issue of personal integrity and the qualifications for Christian ministry. When I questioned whether or not he should continue in the ministry after a third divorce, he said rather indignantly, "I have had a 'Samuel anointing' on my life since my mother's womb." He blindly believed that he has a lifelong ministry license and that multiple divorces, dysfunctional marriages, and other personal failures in no way disqualified him from ministry.

As long as enough of us are careless and clueless, unaccountable and unscrupulous ministers will continue to find places to minister, (1 Timothy 3:2-7) and the devil will continue to divide churches and ministry groups.

Not long ago a pastor caught in an adulterous affair and forced to leave his job asked us (during the process of his job termination), "If you two have forgiven me, God has forgiven me, and this church has forgiven me, then why can't I continue to serve as pastor?"

"The reason is simple," we explained. "You are not currently biblically qualified to be a pastor. Forgiven? Yes. Qualified? No. God says that an elder must be "... *above reproach... temperate, self-controlled, respectable... He must have a good reputation with outsiders, so that he will not fall into disgrace and into the devil's trap*" (1 Timothy 3:2-10). It's clear, from reading the verses following, that he would not even qualify to serve as a deacon in the church!

An apostle, prophet, pastor, teacher, or evangelist in his condition would need to repent, and step down for a season of restoration. That could be for several years. He or she would need to take time to focus on their personal life, their relationship with Christ, and the needs of their family. Mentors are models. A person who is not in right relationship with God and family is in no position to mentor or be a model to the Body of Christ. It requires time to reestablish one's lost credibility.

Leader, if you have been a "covenant breaker" in the past, you are not without hope. Chuck Pierce tells us how you can establish a deeper covenant with God in his book entitled, *Possessing Your Inheritance.*

"As I described earlier," Chuck writes, "many times we don't see the fulfillment of our blessings because we don't keep covenant with God. Refusing to keep covenant with Him will postpone His blessings because we have moved out from under the protection of that covenant where Satan can steal from us.

Refusing to keep our covenants with others, however, can also be a huge opening to the enemy in our lives.

If you have had any covenant-breaking events in your life, including divorce, adultery, broken promises or not completing what you have started, take a moment to repent of any sin you may have committed by doing so. Then ask the Lord to break the power of any covenant-breaking spirits or mind-sets off of you and your family."[6]

Again, if this includes you, then begin to walk in accountability and purity of heart today. A broken man or woman who's been properly restored, and walks in accountability, can be a powerful example of the redemption of Christ.

Key ministry leaders, including prayer ministry leaders, need to remain accountable. For example, prayer groups that operate without pastoral or apostolic authority are set up for future problems.

One godly Christian attorney, himself an intercessor, called to say that he and a group of others from various churches were gathering each week in his home for prayer. When I (Eddie) asked him who was leading the meetings, he explained that they had all agreed that no one would be *in charge*. I told him that anything without a head is a monster. A "headless" group is setting itself up for disappointment.

Sure enough, a few weeks later he called back to explain that someone with less than honorable motives had infiltrated their group and was teaching error. Since no one in the group was recognized as the leader, no one felt authorized to offer direction or to bring correction. The group felt vulnerable and soon dissipated from lack of clear leadership. Some infiltrators are sincere, but they are sincerely wrong!

Accountability in ministry is crucial. It is very important in prophetic ministry for sure. Perhaps no other area can do as much damage as quickly as can prophetic ministry run amuck. The following chapters we'll consider some problem areas and how we have sought to solve them.

Chapter Ten
First Person Prophecies

- ## Leadership failure

The first reason prophetic ministry disappoints is when leaders fail to lead. If you are a leader, we again encourage you to write and publish your guidelines on how prophecy will work in your church or ministry.

A second reason prophetic ministries go sour is when the guidelines aren't followed. Guidelines provide safety for the group, the leader and perhaps most importantly for the person who receives the prophecy. I (Alice) have been in those prayer and prophecy settings where anything goes. It's often total chaos. Paul offers some very specific rules for corporate gatherings in 1 Corinthians 14.

- ## "First person" prophesies

We encourage Christians not to share prophetic words in the *Old Testament, first person* format. Instead, we suggest that they interpret what they *feel* or *sense* the Lord is saying.

For example, rather than say, "Thus saith the Lord, 'I am this or I am that...'" We feel it's more appropriate to humbly say, "I *believe* the Lord *might* be saying to us this or that..." We say this for two reasons.

First, the prophecy may be incorrect. Even the most anointed and experienced prophet among us will miss it at times. The apostle Paul, who wrote much of the New Testament, recognized his own limitations when hearing from and speaking for God. He said that we all *"prophesy in part"* and *"see through a glass darkly."* (1 Corinthians 13:9, 12)

Paul also taught that prophetic revelations are to be judged. (1 Corinthians 2:15; 14:32). So, when we interpret the word, and present it graciously in a spirit of humility, we leave room for the hearer(s) to judge whether or not they believe the word is from God. By the way, it may be an accurate word that the hearer *doesn't* receive. That's okay. The Lord will reveal it at the right time.

Secondly, some argue that since the Old Testament prophets spoke in the first person for God, we should also. Let's remember that the Old Testament prophets were the ones through whom the Holy Spirit spoke to the people.

However, in the New Testament Body of Christ, the Holy Spirit indwells *every* member. Therefore, each member is expected to hear God's voice, and to judge every word of prophecy for him- or herself. (1 Corinthians 2:12-16; 14:32)

The Old Testament prophet was <u>the</u> *voice of God*; the New Testament prophet is only <u>a</u> *voice for God*, since His sheep (that's us), also hear His voice.

- **Archaic language**

No doubt you've noticed that six-hundred-year-old Elizabethan English isn't generally spoken in the 21st Century. Hey, prophets and prophetesses, speak the language of the people. Jesus did! He was a common man who spoke with fishermen. Why should you shift to King James' *"thees and thous"* when you talk to the Lord, or when you speak for the Lord? Are we to assume that God isn't aware that no one talks like that today?

Perhaps one reason a prophetic person might speak in first person and King James English is to validate their message. After all, how can anyone question a word that sounds as though it were spoken by a "King James Version—Old Testament" prophet? Problem is, they spoke Hebrew, not King James

English. The bottom line is that the Holy Spirit doesn't need validation. Moreover, anything we do in an attempt to validate ourselves, or our messages, only proves that we feel invalid, crippled, or inadequate. Be real, and the Lord will use you powerfully.

- **Inaccurate messages**

Perhaps you heard about the man who stood to prophesy one night saying (of course in the first person), "As I, the Lord your God, said to my prophet Jeremiah, or was it Isaiah?" (Are we to conclude that God gets so confused He can't remember what He's saying, or to whom He said it? ☺

Then there was the lady who prophesied (again, in the first person), "I, the Lord thy God, saith unto thee, my people. Because of thy sin, I have written 'Michelob' over the door of this church." She meant to say "Ichabod," which in Hebrew means, *the Lord has departed."* (1 Samuel 4:21) (Michelob® is a popular brand of beer in the United States…or so we're told.)

Finally, one man stood and prophesied, "I, the Lord God, am grieved. My Spirit hath departed this place." An elderly man in the middle of the congregation was heard to mutter, "Then who's doin' the talkin'?"

Come on… don't get all out of sorts. Most of us have heard of, or have experienced some prophetic messes. Again, we prefer that prophetic words be shared in a way that graciously allows the hearers to arrive at their own conclusions.

We like what our friend Dutch Sheets said in *Intercessory Prayer* about the prophetic.

> "Check with godly and mature leaders before doing anything of a public nature or something that seems extremely strange. Don't take your cue from the prophet Isaiah and run around town naked (he probably wore a loincloth). Use wisdom and when in doubt, always check it out. If that isn't possible, then in doubt, don't. Never do anything that contradicts Scripture or might bring reproach on the name of the Lord."[7]

Chapter Eleven
What about False Prophecies?

One line of logic commonly heard among those who reject prophetic ministry says, "A prophet who makes one mistake is a false prophet, and should be stoned to death." This argument is based upon a misreading of Deuteronomy 18:20, which says: *"But the prophet, which shall presume to speak a word in my name, which I have not commanded him to speak… even that prophet shall die."* It's not an instruction to kill anyone. It was a warning that one will die.

In the verses that precede this verse, Deuteronomy 13:1-11, an illustration is given of a false prophet that prophesies accurately, but in doing so counsels the people to rebel in their hearts against the Lord. Verse 10 says, *"So you shall stone him to death because he has sought to seduce you from the Lord your God who brought you out from the land of Egypt, out of the house of slavery."* You see it was not the accuracy or inaccuracy of the prophecy that determined a false prophet. The definition of a false prophet was one whose intention was to seduce God's people.

Do you agree that even a false prophet can prophesy accurately at times? Their personal *character*, the intentions of their hearts, along with *the source* of their prophecy (whether it is God, their flesh, or the devil) is what makes them false. The man in this Scripture reference received the death penalty for *counseling the people to rebel against God*! A true prophet exhorts, encourages, warns with love, corrects with grace so the hearer is changed by God. A false prophet creates fear, condemns, and discourages the receiver from seeking more of God.

As we've seen in the case of verse 20, it does not say that he is to be stoned or that anyone for that matter should put him to death. It simply says *he shall die*. Remember, we don't execute adulterers, or delinquent teens today. Do we? We who have experienced God's grace are to extend His grace!

Apparently, some have forgotten that God, who killed sinners in the Old Testament, died for them in the New Testament. Unfortunately, legalistic Christians love *spiritual law enforcement* too much to make good New Testament believers. Legalism has never drawn a lost soul to Christ, and it never will. Love does! *"Above all, love each other deeply, because love covers over a multitude of sins"* (1 Peter 4:8).

What about False Prophecies?

Think about it. When preaching a sermon, if a pastor (who should speak for God) inadvertently says something that isn't true; or gives faulty pastoral counsel to someone, should he be put to death? Nonsense! Yet some pastors place expectations on prophetic ministers that they would never allow to be placed on themselves. The truth is, we all blow it at times!

Should we measure a person's gift by isolating and amplifying one poor example? Which of us would want someone to measure our preaching or leadership by one of our poorest moments? We wouldn't. After all, at our best, we all *"see through a glass darkly;"* and we *"prophesy in part."* It's a matter of common sense mixed with common courtesy. A prophet, as well as a pastor or anyone in leadership with integrity will admit and apologize for his or her failure. A good rule to follow is to seek confirmations, and hold loosely what they feel that God might be saying.

A great article by Jennifer LeClaire, a news editor at Charisma Magazine, is entitled: *The Danger of Presumptuous Prophets*. Jennifer writes:

"Many of you have heard the story of Henry Stanley, the ambitious

Prophetic Integrity

American reporter who went to the Dark Continent in search of Dr. David Livingstone, a 19th-century missionary who explored sub-Saharan Africa.

When Stanley finally tracked down the famed evangelist, his first words when approaching the only other white man in Ujiji, Africa, were, as the story goes, 'Dr. Livingstone, I presume?' The white man's identity may have seemed like a no-brainer to the young journalist, but if he had been a prophet, Stanley's presumption would have landed him in a heap of trouble. That's because presumption is on God's blacklist.

What does it literally mean to presume? And what exactly is presumption? Webster defines presume as 'to form an opinion from little or no evidence,' and 'to take as true or as fact without actual proof.' Presumptuous is defined as *'to overstep due bounds'* and *'to take liberties.'* Those definitions outline some critical prophetic dos and don'ts.

What about False Prophecies?

First off, there is no room for personal opinion in the prophetic. Our 'proof' must come from the Holy Spirit, not our own spirits or some other spirit. As mouthpieces for God, others take our words and insights very seriously. We dare not abuse the grace people perceive on our lives.

We must not fall into the trap of filtering prophetic utterances through our own biases and in doing so deceive the hearers. What would cause the prophet to think anyone wants his opinion, anyway? (We'll get to that in a minute.) The function of the prophet is to reveal the mind and the will of God, not the mind and will of the prophet.

Second, prophets must recognize boundaries and not take the liberty of overstepping their prophetic authority. Yes, where the Spirit of the Lord is, there is liberty, but not the liberty to speak outside our God-given spiritual jurisdiction.

That jurisdiction begins in the local church and expands as the prophet matures. Doubtless, God hates presumption—and He has good reason. There are several variations of the Greek word presume. Typically, the word portrays insolence (insultingly contemptuous speech or conduct), pride, arrogance, or audacity (bold or arrogant disregard for normal restraints). Considering that the Lord includes a proud look and a false witness among the seven abominations, presumption is not something to be taken lightly.

In fact, while the Bible only mentions the words presume, presumed, presumptuous and presumptuously 11 times, it almost always leads to death. Indeed, there are few things worse than a presumptuous prophet. Deuteronomy 18:20 declares, *'The prophet who presumes to speak a word in my name, which I have not commanded him to speak, or who speaks in the name of other gods, that prophet shall die'* (NKJV).

Mercy! Of course, we are living in a time of grace and even the most presumptuous prophet probably won't be struck dead for this sin. But we must ask ourselves: What is happening inside of us, in our spirits, when we presume. Selah"[8]

Chapter Twelve
New Testament Prophecy: An Invitation, or a Declaration?

A prophetic word, either given or received, should be seen as an invitation *from* God, not a declaration *of* God. As a rule, our suggestion is to hold it loosely and wait for confirmations. Hebrews 2:3 teaches that the words which God speaks are to be confirmed. Deuteronomy 19:15 teaches that things are established by two or three witnesses.

Consider Carefully

To receive and deliver a word from the Lord properly is not always a simple task. There are many voices to be heard. Although we should always listen for a word from the Lord, don't forget that the world, the flesh, and the devil all clamor for our attention too. The world, our culture, and our flesh, bring to bear mental impressions and prejudices.

Some revelations, dreams, or visions are only the result of indigestion from the spicy food we ate the night before. Hey, we Texans have the most prolific dreams following our super-deluxe Mexican dinners, loaded with chopped onions and Jalapeno peppers. Yum!

The next consideration is the devil. Demons are often noisy. Unlike God, who speaks only *when and to whom He chooses, and always to glorify His Son,* demons will speak to just about anyone who'll listen. A junior high school student can quickly tap into "the second heaven" and receive a demonic revelation. As mentioned earlier, the three heavens to which Paul referred in 2 Corinthians 12:2 include the first heaven (which we can see); the second heaven (where the Prince and Power of the Air (Satan and his demonic kingdom operate); and the third heaven, where God is. Our goal is to hear from God, not to receive a demonic message from the second heaven, which is the operating realm of psychics and fortunetellers.

Effective communication with Jesus and the ability to distinguish His voice from other voices requires that we become familiar with His Word, pursue holiness, and live with an open ear to Him. When we are rightly related to the Lord, and engaged in ministry awaiting a word from Him, we've learned that the first word that crosses our minds is usually from Him.

New Testament Prophecy: An Invitation, or a Declaration?

I (Eddie) received a call one day from a woman in Dallas. She was a drug addict and alcoholic; and she was at her wit's end. She asked if she could drive down to Houston (4.5 hours) for pastoral counseling. I agreed, and we made the appointment.

My approach is to schedule the counseling session 30 minutes early. I do that to prepare. I prepare by finding a quiet place and sitting in the presence of the Lord, to meditate. (Don't let that word throw you. Psalm 19:14 instructs us to meditate.) I usually ask Him if there is anything He wishes to show me that would help the person I'm about to meet. If so, I write down what I see, hear, or feel.

Sometimes He says nothing. Sometimes He speaks quickly and quite clearly. However, this day, it was 20 minutes before I sensed anything at all. I saw a fleeting mental image (eyes closed) of a pair of women's dancing cowboy boots. Then they were gone. I asked the Holy Spirit what that was about. He impressed on my heart that I was to ask her about the country western dance.

She walked in and sat down. Almost the first thing she said was, "What do you want to know about me?"

"Nothing," I replied. "Don't tell me anything, it will only confuse me," I said, a bit tongue in cheek.

Surprised, she said, "If you don't know anything about me, how can you help me?" She was apparently used to counselors who had her fill out an entire questionnaire so they could determine an approach to consider.

"That's just it," I explained with a smile. "I can't help you. If God, who knows everything about you, doesn't speak to me, you may have just wasted a trip to Houston. He told me to ask you about the country western dance."

She gasped with shock. Tears welled up in her eyes. Then this lovely lady shared with me about the wonderful day she met Christ as a teenager. Two weeks after she was saved, a friend invited her to a country western club. At first, she refused, explaining that she was a new Christian. She already knew that a club wasn't where the Lord wanted her to be. But her determined friend was relentless, and she finally agreed to go.

Late that Saturday night, as she entered the ladies' room, she ran into her Sunday School teacher, who staggered out of the restroom drunk. That moment, she swore she would never attend church again… and she hadn't. Now, she was "the drunk." (Matthew 7:2)

After a time of prayer, as God healed her heart, she repented and was restored in her relationship with the Lord.

All of that was the result of a fleeting vision — prophetic revelation.

The Four Phases of Prophetic Revelation

A prophetic revelation involves four phases. If we miss any one of them, we've missed it.

Do you remember the story of Peter's rooftop dream at noon in Joppa, Israel? Having visited Israel when the temperature exceeded 100 degrees Fahrenheit, we assure you that to be on a rooftop at noon is enough for anyone to run the risk of a heat stroke and accompanying hallucinations! However, Acts 10:9-34 records both Peter's dream and its interpretation. Let's analyze his experience. The four phases of every revelation are: *the revelation* itself, *the interpretation, the application,* and *the assignment* (if any).

1. **The Revelation** *(The Content). What exactly did I dream, did I see, or did I hear? What is God's message?*

Prophetic Integrity

In Peter's dream, a large sheet, held by its corners was lowered to the Earth. On it were all kinds of four-footed animals, reptiles, and birds. Three times God said: *"Get up, Peter. Kill them and eat them."* How could that possibly be God? Peter was a Jew. Jews didn't eat unclean animals. This was against everything in his Jewish upbringing. That was *the revelation.*

2. **The Interpretation** *(The Meaning). What does this mean? What do I feel emotionally? What are my first impressions?*

Peter needed a proper interpretation. What was he to think? An interpretation may come immediately, but that didn't happen in Peter's case. He didn't have a clue. We often see well-meaning Christians move too quickly, jump to conclusions, misinterpret, and apply what they think God has said to them, only to truly mess up. Be patient.

Verse 17 says, *"While Peter was <u>wondering</u> about the meaning of the vision..."* Verse 19 says, *"While Peter was <u>still thinking</u> about the vision..."*

Peter had to "sleep on it." He certainly ran the risk of losing his reputation if what he saw wasn't right. Had he rushed, he might have wrongly

100

concluded it was God's way of telling him to eat rattlesnake meat! Which I (Eddie) understand tastes like chicken. ☺ It's an odd message and another reminder that although God spoke to Moses face-to-face, He speaks to us, as He did that day to Peter, in riddles. (Numbers 12:8)

The next day God revealed to Peter the interpretation of his dream. In verse 28 Peter says to a large gathering of people, *"You are well aware that it is against our law for a Jew to associate with a Gentile or visit him. But God has shown me that I should not call any man impure or unclean."*

Then in verse 34 he says, *"I now realize how true it is that God does not show favoritism but accepts men from every nation who fear him and do what is right…"*

Each of us would do well to "sleep on it" when it comes to interpretation. Improper timing can be as bad as an incorrect word. Immature prophets or intercessors will often speak prematurely. Let's wait for God to reveal the interpretation before we act. We can trust Him!

In the same way, immature hearers will prematurely act on the prophetic words given to them. We have received prophetic words that weren't fulfilled for months, some even years later. The longer you walk with Jesus, the more you can understand how He communicates with you personally.

2. The Application *(The Enactment). How and when does this occur?*

Had Peter immediately marched off, even with the correct revelation and interpretation, to evangelize Gentiles (non-Jews) without waiting for God's directions, Cornelius and his family might never have been saved. As he waited for the Lord to direct his next step, the Holy Spirit led Peter to Cornelius' house in Caesarea, which resulted in a great harvest of souls! (Acts 10:19; Acts 10:44-48)

3. The Assignment *(Sharing). When (if ever) and to whom (if anyone) are we to share what we feel God is saying.*

In verses 28 and 29 Peter shares his dream and its meaning. Those who seem to hear best from the Lord are often the most hesitant to immediately share what they've heard. Why? It's because credibility and obedience are more important than attention. Paul certainly knew that tension. Notice what he says in 2 Corinthians 12:1-4,

"I must go on boasting. Although there is nothing to be gained, I will go on to visions and revelations from the Lord. 2 I know a man in Christ, who fourteen years ago was caught up to the third heaven. Whether it was in the body or out of the body I do not know — God knows. 3 And I know that this man — whether in the body or apart from the body I do not know, but God knows — 4 was caught up to paradise and heard inexpressible things, things that no one is permitted to tell."

Randy, (not his real name) a friend of mine (Alice) in the real estate business, called one day for counsel. He said that he didn't know why the prophecies given to him, and his wife, hadn't been fulfilled.

"We pray every day for them to come to pass. We are doing everything we can, to make them happen. So, what's wrong?"

At that moment I felt like the Holy Spirit gave me a word of knowledge, not only for Randy and his family, but for all the "Randy's" in the greater Christian community who are prophecy-driven.

"Randy," I said. "The reason the prophecies aren't coming to pass is because you are focused on

103

them—and not on the Lord. The fact that you are striving for the fulfillment of prophecies given you, reveals that you aren't yet ready to receive. You have yet to surrender, and to let go of the agenda, and submit to God's timing. Ecclesiastes 3:11a KJV says, *"He hath made all things beautiful <u>in his time</u>…"*

Once you forget about the prophetic word and strive to be like Jesus—your answer will come. You'll see your breakthrough!"

Most of the revelations God gives us relates to personal prayer assignments. I (Alice) stated in my book *Beyond the Veil* that most mature intercessors reveal no more than 20% of what God shows them, and hold 80% in secret.

In the last twenty years, Christian leaders have begun to believe the Church is at the threshold of experiencing the fulfillment of Joel 2:28, *"And afterward, I will pour out my Spirit on all people. Your sons and daughters will prophesy, your old men will dream dreams, your young men will see visions."* Since that's the case, pastors, prayer leaders, and other ministry leaders should provide safe learning environments for them in preparation for a mighty prophetic outpouring.

We generally discourage people from sharing directional and correctional prophetic words with others. These include words like, "God told me He wants you to quit your job and look for another;" or "God said you are wrong about…" What does the Bible say? We are told, *"But everyone who prophesies speaks to men for their strengthening, encouragement and comfort"* (1 Corinthians 14:3). So, the most honoring of prophets will use their gift to *strengthen, to encourage,* and *to comfort* fellow believers; and never for self-aggrandizement, control or to manipulate others.

Good leaders establish boundaries. If any of your people have words of edification, encouragement, or comfort for someone we suggest that you develop your own system and instruct them as to how they are to share their insights. However, if they have a negative word, we suggest intercessory prayer as their first step. Only mature, experienced believers should ever administer directive or corrective words; and that with the right heart attitude, positioned under proper spiritual authority. (Galatians 6:1)

Immature Christians sometimes seek to "notch their prophetic gun handles" by correctly predicting the sex of an unborn baby. As a rule, prophetic people should resist the urge to do so unless you are instructed by the Lord. After all, even a chimpanzee has a 50/50 chance being right, doesn't he? ☺ It is sad to see the disappointment brought upon young parents who have been misdirected by what proves to be an incorrect and generally unnecessary prophecy (prediction). I (Alice) made this mistake in the mid 80s when a couple in our home group, who were already blessed with a little girl, wanted a baby boy.

One night in our group I prophesied over Robin that she would have a baby boy. Well, a month or so later, she was pregnant and we were so sure that the baby was a boy. Based on my prophecy, she and her husband painted their nursery blue, and bought clothes and furniture for the arrival of their new son. You can only imagine their shock and ours when she gave birth to another beautiful little girl.

I profusely apologized to them and to our cell group. Thankfully, I have grown in the prophetic since the 1980s. Sure. Like you, I still miss it at times… and guess what? So will you. Even if you are confident about your word on the sex of a baby, should you tell them, it might be wise to encourage them to hold the word loosely.

The late John and Paula Sandford in their book, *The Elijah Task*, give us instruction about using care with the prophetic.

"Prophets should not only be careful how they hear the Lord; they also need to learn that people's wishes can affect their hearing. One friend called me, long distance, in great consternation. 'My son just took off with three friends to fly from Seattle to Sun Valley. A squall came up. They haven't been heard from. Search planes are up. Can you give us a word from God?' We need to be careful not to be placed in the position of seers or wizards. Saul thought Samuel was a seer who could tell him where to find his lost asses. This is not the primary function of a prophet. (1 Samuel 9:9) But my friend wanted to know where her son was. So I asked the Lord anyway. The answer was immediate. They had flown north, not south, and were lost. There was no hope. I tried as gently as I could to tell her over the phone. Unbeknownst to me, the woman had such confidence in me, she persuaded the searchers to switch the operation to cover the northern area indicated. Then she called me again and again. Her importunity worked upon me and then upon my clarity with God. I began to think the Lord was telling me good news through various visions, which I passed on to my friend. I was not sufficiently aware how our connections with others in our spirit can affect our channel with God. The next summer, when the snow melted, the crashed plane was found, in the area I had first indicated. The falling snow had immediately hidden it. The four had died instantly."[9]

If a seasoned proven prophet like John Sandford could be persuaded to revise his word, how much more careful should we be? Why are some leaders reluctant, even fearful to acknowledge and release revelatory ministry? For some, it is because of their lack of knowledge or inexperience. We are all a bit reluctant to deal with something new.

Face it. Pastors are busy people. To learn and develop a new area of ministry isn't easy. For one thing, leaders are reluctant to share things about which they have no hands-on experience. For another, written and recorded equipping resources like this book differ widely. In addition to that, it requires skill, time, and considerable prayer to lead an entire congregation in a new direction. Being a pastor is no easy responsibility.

For others, it's because of a past painful experience with the prophetic, or a result of horror stories they've heard where leadership failed, or where a receiver was embarrassed, humiliated, or wounded in the process. We've certainly heard enough of those stories.

Finally, there are some who simply refuse to assume the responsibility to oversee it. To them, it's one less problem with which they have to deal. However, think of all the lives that could be potentially changed with a prophetic word given at the right time in the right way. Of course, pastors would have to train, or to provide training for the prophetically gifted people in their congregations.

For the pastor who feels led to stretch into these areas, we would suggest, unless otherwise led by the Lord that you start small and move slowly. Began with a handful of people.

Chapter Thirteen
Picking Up the Prophetic Pieces

Attention Pastor:
How to shepherd your flock in the wake of
unfulfilled prophetic words.

A non-profit ministry asked a well-known speaker to receive an offering for the ministry during one of its gatherings. After taking the microphone, the man announced to the group, "The Lord told me before I left my hotel tonight that tonight's offering tonight will be $225,000! Can I hear an 'amen'?" The loyal crowd, of course, resounded with a hearty "amen!"

As soon as the offering was collected, the overly confident guest speaker insisted that it be counted so they could celebrate the result. When it was reported that the offering from approximately 500 people was roughly $34,000, the prophet berated the people for their unfaithfulness to the Lord and their failure to hear and obey Him. The hosts, grateful for what they felt was a generous, heartfelt offering, were horrified, yet unwilling to embarrass their guest by stopping him publicly.

Prophetic Integrity

The man chided the people for a few more minutes, then ordered another offering as a second chance to "obey the Lord." When only an additional $6,000 was received, the indignant speaker sat down with disgust.

(Let's pause for a moment. Wouldn't this have been a good time to graciously say, "Thank you folks for the generosity you have shown this ministry. I clearly missed what I felt the amount would be.")

Following the event, the hosts were overwhelmed with calls from pastors to business people who were upset, and some confused, by the speaker's behavior. The hosts forwarded some of the complaints to the speaker to ask for an explanation; and for his instruction on how they should handle the matter. He never acknowledged their concern, answered their correspondence, or apologized to them. He ignored it all.

From the failed Y2K disaster prophecies; to "Jesus is coming back on September 20th;" to "God told me He's going to heal everyone here tonight with back trouble;" congregations and individuals often feel betrayed and dishonored by thoughtless prophets.

Countless pastors have been burned by itinerant ministers who've rolled into town, dished out grand prophecies, and then have conveniently left the pastors to deal with the messy aftermath. Their natural instinct is to reject it, become cynical, and closed to further involvement with the prophetic—at least for a period of time.

Yet the prophetic gifts, when used humbly, under the guidance of the Holy Spirit, can usher in the blessings of God. Even the Apostle Paul warns us not to "despise prophecies" (1 Thessalonians 5:20). But is that possible for pastors whose people have been injured, even abused, by misguided "words from the Lord"? What can leaders do to pick up the pieces?

Don't Throw the Baby Out with the Bathwater

Resolution often begins with a reminder. And in the case of questioning the overall purpose of prophecy after a misguided prophet hurts your congregation, it helps to remember God's original intention for this beautiful but powerful gift. A pastor's nature is to protect the sheep, which is why some leaders respond to major "prophetic messes" by shutting down prophetic ministry altogether. It's understandable, yet unnecessarily extreme.

Keep in mind that the gift of prophecy is the only gift that appears in all three "gift lists": Romans 12; 1 Corinthians 12; and Ephesians 4. God has called each of us to prophesy (1 Corinthians 14:5, 39; Acts

2:17-21). This supernatural expression of the Holy Spirit is to be a natural experience of every believer. For this to be so, we must sincerely desire to prophesy (1 Corinthians 14:1) and be equipped as we would be for any other ministry.

Prophecy isn't an optional ministry; it's essential for equipping the church (Ephesians 4:11-12). To forbid it is to undermine the very foundation of the church (Ephesians 2:20). Delivered in the right way, at the right time, in the right spirit, a prophetic word can be used by God to bring healing, restoration and deliverance. It can set churches and people in order, and it can evangelize the lost.

One day I (Alice) went to a diner to have breakfast. Eddie was out of town so I decided to eat out before I ran my errands. As I walked into the diner I saw a middle-aged woman who was apparently one of the waitresses. I sensed by the Holy Spirit that she was confused, upset and financially strapped. Even though she was smiling on the outside, I knew in my spirit that she felt alone and trapped. I can't tell you how I knew, I just knew. As I sat down, I began to pray in my heart for the Lord's wisdom and assignment.

As she stepped to my table, I ordered breakfast, then I said, "Ma'am, I don't know you but I know Jesus Christ knows you perfectly. I feel He wants me to share a few things with you. Are you okay with this?" She nodded her head "yes," as tears welled up in her eyes.

"I believe the Lord Jesus told me that you are in a terrible predicament. That you are hurt, shocked, and worried. I feel He said that your husband has walked out on you, and without job skills you are financially unable to provide for the needs of your family." Now she was crying so hard that she was attracting the attention of several customers in nearby tables.

She told me that her husband had left her and their four children for a younger woman the day before. I didn't care that I was in a diner. I reached for her hand and began to pray for comfort, peace and provision. After my prayer, there was a holy hush in the restaurant. (Honestly, I had prayed very quietly, but the Holy Spirit's presence had settled over the entire restaurant). It was a precious moment I will never forget.

At the end of my meal the waitress hugged and thanked me for the encouraging words. She said she knew now that Jesus Christ was going to help her. I slipped a $200 check into her hands before I left. Eddie was in an airplane so I couldn't get an agreement, but I knew he would have done the same. I suspect that I wasn't the only patron in that small diner that day to give to that sweet woman in need.

Proceed with Parameters

There is, of course, the negative side of prophecy that can be destructive. Even the early church had a problem with the prophetic. Yet Paul warned them that to despise the prophetic is to quench the Holy Spirit. He told them not to be gullible, but to test every good word and hold on to the truth (1 Thessalonians 5:19-21). Or as the proverb says, "Eat the fish and spit out the bones."

If the prophetic comes with a few potential problems, why embrace it? Why provide training, and publish guidelines for the prophetic? Because there will never be a day when you or your people don't need to be built up, encouraged and comforted (1 Corinthians 14:3). We live in difficult days and can expect even harder times ahead. People need the confirmation, edification, exhortation and encourage-ment the prophetic provides.

Here are some suggested guidelines for words of knowledge and prophecy. Consider them as you develop your own.

1. If prophetic words are allowed in a public worship service, consider designating a pastoral staff member to

hear them and grant permission before they're shared publicly. Some churches establish a prophetic council for this purpose. The word may not be from the Lord or the timing may not be right.

It's true that some prophetic types will view this as "pastoral control," and reason that no one approves the pastor's sermons—why should their words require approval? They confuse their role with that of the pastor's. They overlook the pastor's authority and responsibility. God doesn't hold the prophet accountable for the pastor's sermons, but He does hold the pastor accountable for the prophetic words that he allows to be spoken into the lives of his people.

2. Design a "revelatory form" that a member can pick up and fill out. One of the churches we served had a box on the wall outside the church offices into which prophetic words could be placed. The printed forms, include a place for their names, telephone numbers, email

addresses and the date. There were small boxes they could check to indicate whether theirs was a dream, a prophetic word, a vision, or a Scripture. They were to write the word they'd received and explain their interpretation (if they had one), along with how they thought it should be applied.

Explain to your people that once they place the completed form in the locked drop box outside the office, other than to pray, their assignment is finished. The pastoral/ministry staff will pray about the revelation, seeking God's confirmation and direction.

3. Encourage those who prophesy not to give directional words to individuals in your church or ministry without leadership approval. Especially if they are new believers or novices in prophecy. (These would be words such as "quit your job," "sell your house," "divorce your spouse," etc.) Remember, the primary purpose of prophecy is to build up, encourage, and comfort one another.

Speak Up!

Pastor, if you are uneasy about a prophetic word given to your congregation, stand up and say so. The longer you wait, the more it will cost you. Say something like: "We should each judge the prophetic word just given to us. Let's submit what we've heard to the Lord and ask Him to clarify and confirm it if it's truly from Him."

We're convinced that greater damage has been done from pastoral failure to correct prophetic abuses than from prophetic abuses. If you, as a leader, hear a word being offered in the wrong timing or in the wrong spirit, then gently interrupt the speaker. You might softly say, "I feel that this word isn't for us at this time, thank you." By doing this, you communicate how much you love your people. Most prophetic problems could be avoided—or at least quickly resolved—if pastors and prophets had relationships of honor, respect, and accountability.

It's also crucial that prophets understand their place in the Body of Christ. When we were pastors, we made sure that our people knew that "*none* of us is as important as *all* of us." It is better that you err on the side of protecting the sheep, than protecting the prophet.

Prophetic Integrity

If your people have been wounded by a prophetic word, don't sweep it under the carpet. That only communicates your lack of leadership. Instead, in a private setting lovingly explain that we (including the one who wounded them) are all saved sinners, prone to error. We are all growing in the prophetic, and will miss the mark at times. Even if you weren't the one who disappointed them, apologize for the misuse of the gift.

Certainly, this approach would be for an extreme case. Let's not go overboard, lest this attempt to correct things does more harm than the misplaced word.

We leaders, who purport to speak for God, should do so thoughtfully and humbly; and encourage those who receive prophecies to offer grace and forgiveness when others—including us—disappoint.

When I (Eddie) was a pastor, I encouraged our members to put a box of forgiveness for me in their hearts. "I'm certain that from time to time, I will be making withdrawals."

Matthew 24 warns us that in the end times, false prophets will lead people astray and even deceive the elect, if possible. Be discerning, accountable and weigh every word, purportedly from God, by the written

Word of God. James encourages us to ask the Lord for wisdom. As leaders, we would do well to follow his advice. Because in the tumultuous days ahead, proper use of the prophetic will have a powerful impact on cutting-edge churches and ministries that steward it correctly.

Helping Your Church Heal from Prophetic Abuse

There's no quick fix when it comes to recovering from a damaging, misguided prophecy. Yet here are a few steps to take as you lead people through the aftermath.

1. Repent for the prophetic abuse. Even if you're blameless, consider "identificational repentance" on behalf of those involved. You can do this without condemning or demeaning the prophet. (Explain that leaders, like everyone else, are prone to error too. Then express your sorrow for the matter.) Identification prayer is simply agreeing that, except for the grace of God, any of us are prone to give incorrect prophecy.

2. Tell them exactly how they should view the person who delivered the misguided word. For example: "He was sincere, but as your leader, I feel his word was misguided. We all miss it from time to time, and we learn from our mistakes." Of course, if the event was more grievous, a more serious and direct explanation may be required.

3. Explain the importance of forgiving, and lead them to forgive. Remind them of Jesus' parable on forgiveness in Matthew 18, where a man owed his king a fortune that he could never pay. Then when his king forgave the debt, refused to forgive a small debt a man owed him.

Hearing about it, the king ordered the man to be incarcerated and turned over to "the tormentors." Then, Jesus said, "This is what the Heavenly Father, who has forgiven us, will do with us if we refuse to forgive those who sin against us." NOTE: *If you need additional insight, I (Eddie) devote two chapters in my book,* 10 Steps to Freedom, *to cover the topic in much greater detail. That book is available here. www.PrayerBookstore.com*

4. Lead them in a prayer to bless the prophet who offended them.

"Father, thank You for your mercy. You tell us that "mercy triumphs over judgment" (James 2:13). As You are merciful to me, I now offer mercy and forgiveness to ___name___, who offended me. Thank You for loving us, even when we fail You. Teach us to love one another. I love You Lord. In Jesus' name, Amen."

5. Remind them that they are to always judge prophetic words with a heart of gratitude. Warn them that just because this word wasn't on target doesn't mean that every prophetic word from this person is necessarily wrong.

6. Encourage them in the future to

always hold such words loosely, to seek godly counsel, and to await confirmations from the Lord.

7. Pray a pastoral blessing over them.

Like some fathers, who refuse to change their baby's diapers, some spiritual overseers who read this will say, "That does it. I just won't open the door to prophetic gifts." That is exactly what Satan hopes you'll do. He knows the importance of keeping the communication lines down between heaven's troops and their Commanding General! Around the world, Satan's kingdom suffers from the ministry of godly, prophetically gifted Christians who are accountable to spiritual authority. In our book, *Intercessors and Pastors: the Emerging Partnership of Pastors and Intercessors*, we point out how pastors and people of prayer must develop a lasting relationship if we are to see a last day harvest in the earth. Satan knows better than we, the growing importance for the Church to hear God in these last days!

Although God is restoring prophetic ministry to His church worldwide, in most of our churches and ministries across the denominational and nondenominational spectrum, prophetic ministry is still in its infancy. Let's not *"despise the day of small things"* (Zechariah 4:10 KJV). In Proverbs 14:4 we read, *"Where no oxen are, the crib is clean: but much increase is by the strength of the ox."* Surely you get this verse!

Danger can be difficult to deal with. A pastor loves the sheep given to his care. His God-given instinct is to protect them. However, some have lost sight of their second option. They have the option to face the difficulties and to teach their people to hear God. In a *Charisma Magazine* article entitled "Letters," the writer's comment interested us:

> "A pastor from Alabama says, 'My wife and I, as pastors, were involved in the prophetic movement but have now removed ourselves from this camp. We stepped away because we saw abuse of the prophetic. The personal power many of these prophets have over people is too hard to resist. They use their 'words;' to gain position, control and notoriety among Christians… We have confused monetary gain with maturity, we have confused charisma with character, and

we have confused performance with power."[11]

With the problems the prophetic may present at times, especially in its infancy, balanced prophetic ministry benefits the health and ministry of the church.

This presupposes that those engaged in it recognize pastoral authority. As C. Peter Wagner points out in his book, *Prophets and Pastors: Protocol for Healthy Churches*:

> In the local church, a prophet is a member of a team, but not the team's leader...
>
> I like to think of pastors and prophets as pitchers and catchers. When you watch a baseball game, the camera is on the pitchers and catchers the majority of the time. They are not the whole team, but they definitely are the core of the defense. Notice that the pitcher is the authority. The pitcher is the only player who is credited with the win or charged with the loss of the game. In a local church (or ministry), the pastor (or

ministry leader) is the pitcher and the catcher is the prophet.

The catcher gives the signals to the pitcher. But every signal is subject to the final authority of the pitcher. In the great majority of the cases, the pitcher accepts the signals from the catcher and throws accordingly. But sometimes, no. The catcher advises the pitcher, but is also subject to the final authority of the pitcher. Over the years, this baseball protocol has been well developed.[12]

Mature leaders can face these difficulties and still teach their people to hear God's voice. In other words, *they can throw out the bath water,* and keep the baby. Note: the elders (spiritual leaders) are to remain at the gates!

Discerning truth from error will always be a challenge because error is never far from the truth. Jesus explained that the wheat and tares (the saved and the lost) will grow together. (Matthew 13:30). Truth and error are next door neighbors. However, light always overcomes darkness! Truth is never threatened by the presence of error.

Prophetic Integrity

God still speaks today. We are obligated to listen and if necessary, *to learn to listen*. Let's not allow our fear to cause us to fail to obey God's Word.

What's a Leader to Do?

We have had to work through some of these issues in the crucible of personal pastoral experience. Most of it has been sweet, some sour. At times we've wondered why we were chosen to endure such difficulty. The answer is clear. God makes the assignments. If we reject the assignment, we cannot benefit from the knowledge. If we don't benefit from the knowledge, we can't share it with others. We encourage you to identify the spiritually sensitive people in your sphere of influence and begin to disciple them in their gifts.

We have a great prophetic intercessor who has been part of our ministry since the 90s. Carol Pauwels and her husband Alex had been part of a challenging church situation where the pastor's wife was spiritually abusive and demeaning to some of the women in the congregation. As a result, Carol's powerful and amazingly accurate prophetic anointing was crushed, causing her to be scared, wounded and tentative. When she became part of my (Alice) Wednesday morning prayer group, I could tell that she longed for a leader who would love her and gently instruct her in the prophetic.

The challenge was about six months later when Eddie and I along with four other ladies went to teach prophecy at a church that was in transition regarding the things of the Holy Spirit.

After Eddie had taught one of the sessions, he asked the ladies if they had any prophetic words to share with the congregation. It was like a prophetic river, the people were so hungry to hear from the Lord.

Carol was anxious to try out her new prophetic freedom. However, when she received something and asked the person to stand, it was unnerving for the person receiving. From Carol's zeal she virtually exploded with passion and intensity. Her eyes got fiery, her voice raised with authority. It almost appeared she was in a frenzy to deliver her word. By the response of the receiver, the word was right, but her delivery left something to be desired. After the meeting, I sat down with Carol and lovingly shared with her how she came across. Carol is one of the most teachable Christians I know. She said she wanted to receive. Although Carol will always be passionate about the words she gives, she graciously tries to deliver them with a relaxed countenance and a gracious smile.

Encourage Them to Stay Close to the Lord

Holiness and purity are essential qualities for their protection. They simply cannot walk in darkness without walking in deception.

I (Eddie) am fond of something Alice says:

"A pure heart has no conflict of interest. Purity is the outcome of continual exposure to God's presence. A stream is purest near its source. That is why the more time we spend in private devotion to the Lord Jesus, our motives, behavior, and our lifestyle will begin to be more like Him. We are living near the source—Jesus."

Counsel Them to Stay in the Word

Scripture is the acid test for any revelation. The Word of God must be central to our thinking. To wander from its truth is to be led astray. The Lord will never tell us anything contrary to Scripture. The most effective prophet is one who skillfully uses the Word of God along with his or her prophetic word. Learning God's Word doesn't occur overnight. It's not a destination, it's a lifelong process.

Instruct Them to Remain
Submitted to the Body of Christ

The Lord has built checks and balances of accountability into His Body, the Church. We can't walk with God and live separately from His people. Proverbs teaches that there is safety in a multitude of counselors. (Proverbs 11:14) The issue of congregational and pastoral authority is also critical to the prophetic.

Beware of the person who "belongs to several churches." Translated, that means they aren't accountable to any church. Truth is, that person feels he or she is above a need for accountability. If your pastor doesn't affirm you, or doesn't yet appreciate prophetic ministry, pray for him or her. If your pastor's lifestyle is contrary to God's Word, you are likely in the wrong church. Seek God's guidance. Remember, you are a messenger, not a manipulator. Only the Lord can change a heart.

A Faithful Helper

The prophetic ministry can be one of the easiest places for the enemy to infiltrate. But God has not left us alone. He has given us His Holy Spirit to guide us into all truth. *"But when he, the Spirit of truth, comes, he will guide you into all truth. He will not speak on his own; he will speak only what he hears, and he will tell you what is yet to come"* (John 16:13).

Recently I (Eddie) asked a group that I was teaching, "How many of you feel as if you are spiritually deceived at some point?" Less than 5% of them raised their hands. "Interesting," I explained, "I suggest that those of you who did not raise your hands *are* deceived."

I have sermons I once preached that I can no longer preach. Why? I can't preach them because I no longer believe them. If your understanding of yourself, the Father, and His Word haven't grown over the past several years you aren't likely growing in Christ. You are stagnant. Growth demands change.

Let's admit that we don't and we never will know it all. Let's remain flexible and teachable in the hands of God. Let's face potential deception without fear. Our God is trustworthy. Let's place more trust in our Father's ability to protect us more than the enemy's ability to deceive us.

The Holy Spirit is God's agent of revelation, the Spirit who discloses. You see, the One who speaks to us is also the One whose job is to protect us. Let's learn to hear and to trust Him. Will we make mistakes?

Certainly, we will. Progress requires risk. Let's continue to risk and to learn.

Chapter Fourteen
Establish a
Communication System

Jesus didn't say, "My *shepherds* hear my voice" He said, "*My* sheep *hear my voice.*" Leader, teach your people how and when to share their revelations with you. Encourage your prophetically gifted people to write down their dreams, visions, and words for themselves and for you.

At his early service one Sunday morning, one of our friends said that he suddenly realized that he'd preached the worst sermon in his life. He was both humiliated and embarrassed. He would have tried to come up with another sermon for the second service, but there were only 20 minutes between the services. As he walked toward his office a lady church member, anxious to talk with him, stopped him and said, "Pastor, I have a word for you."

He said, "I wanted to put my hand on her forehead and speak commandingly, 'Be raptured in the name of Jesus!' but I didn't. ☺ Instead, I said, 'Thank you, Mary. But I don't need a word right now. I desperately need *an entire sermon!'*"

Prophetic Integrity

Like Mary, well-meaning people can sometimes pick the most inopportune times to bring things to a leader's attention. Let your prophetic people know how much you love and admire them; and provide them with the proper tools with which they can best share with you.

Most importantly, tell your prophetic team what to do with their revelations. How do you want to receive revelatory words? Have you provided a locked box into which they can drop them? Would you like for them to leave the message for you with the church secretary? Would you prefer that they be mailed to your office or home? Perhaps you would like to designate someone to collect the revelatory words, study them, look for duplications and confirmations, pray over them, file them, and submit to you in summary to keep you informed as to what God may to be saying through His body.

Although we strive to be open and available to our team members, unless it's an emergency, we discourage them from interrupting our family's schedule, or confronting us right before we are about to teach or preach. You might wish to do as we did, create a revelatory form.

If you are prophetically gifted, be considerate of your leader's family life and study time. Respect the fact that your Pastor is always "on call" and never "off duty."

When you submit a revelatory word to your pastor or ministry leader, *release it*. Do not insist that he or she act on it. Remember that God speaks to them too. Many leaders receive a steady flow of words like yours. You *may* receive feedback, but don't necessarily expect it. Trust it to the Lord. The larger the organization, the less likely the leaders can respond to every word that is submitted.

Think of it this way. The mail carrier who delivers your bills doesn't return three days later to ask if you've paid them. He is just the delivery person.

Some years ago I (Eddie) was in a large national gathering at one of the largest Southern Baptist Churches in our city. The huge auditorium was packed with several thousand leaders, most of whom were guests in our city. The host pastor was politely making introductions, when a rather odd gentleman near me, stood to his feet, shook his arm in the air, and began to loudly rail against him, "This man doesn't believe in women preachers!"

Recognizing that ushers had not been appointed for this impromptu weekday meeting, and having been a minister in the city for more than 30 years, I jumped up, rushed to where the man was. I took him firmly by the arm, and invited two other men to help me "usher him" out of the auditorium. They did.

Once outside, I asked the man why he had interrupted such an important meeting.

He answered, "Pastor Jim (not his real name) doesn't believe in women preachers and won't allow women to speak from his pulpit."

I asked, "Did God reveal to you that it is okay for women to preach?"

He piously replied, "Yes, indeed!"

"So you DO believe that God still speaks today," I asked.

"Absolutely," he said.

I probed further, "Do you believe that Pastor Jim is a believer?"

He said, "Yes."

I said, "May I then suggest that you trust the God who revealed that to you, to reveal that to Pastor Jim in His time."

By then the man was calm, and we all returned to the auditorium.

Establish a Communication System

We must never confuse information with revelation. No one can be *argued into* receiving revelation.

We keep all of the words our intercessors give us. We file them in several thick, three-ring binders. The words go back many years. It's probable that many of those words weren't divinely inspired. After all, we have spent decades now in the learning mode. Even those words that are from God must pass through our human hearts and minds. Yet, some of the words given to us twenty or more years ago are only now coming to pass. Had we not established our system then, we would not have the advantage of celebrating today's confirmations. Nor would we have been able to recognize and establish a "track record" of their growth in accuracy and maturity in the Lord.

Many years ago, Debbie Walker, one of our personal intercessors, had a word from the Lord for us that has forever changed our lives. Having resigned from our prior church, we didn't have a clue concerning God's direction for our future.

In prayer one day, Debbie sensed that several statements from the movie, *Field of Dreams* applied to us. God does use unusual things to get His points across at times. This was one for sure.

Prophetic Integrity

You may recall that *Field of Dreams* was a story about a young man and his family living on a farm in the Midwestern United States. It was apparent that the star, Roy (played by Kevin Costner), suffered from an unfulfilled dream when his father failed to make it in major league baseball. Instead, his father died with an untrue scandal haunting him.

The plot develops as Roy walks through the middle of his ripened cornfield one day. With near disbelief, he hears a voice whispering the recurring instruction that if he will level a large portion of his corn field and build a lighted, professional baseball diamond the "big league" baseball greats of the past, including his deceased father, will come and play ball there. This would vindicate his father, and the presence of the former baseball stars would draw people to his field from miles around. The phrase that Roy continued to hear was, "If you build it, they will come."

Having read her note, we rented the movie. As a confirming word, along with other words we received, it stirred our faith. Somehow, while we were seeking the Lord's direction for our lives, our faith was strengthened enabling us, at that point to believe there was even greater ministry in our future. Within weeks, we launched the U.S. Prayer Center, which continues to this day with a mission to "disciple nations by equipping Christian leaders.

Recently, the story of another baseball great, Jackie Robinson, has been portrayed on the big screen in the Hollywood movie, "42." Jackie was the first black man to play major league baseball with (at that time) the Brooklyn Dodgers. His is the story of victory over endemic societal racism to become a baseball legend!

Perhaps you have faced opposition to your prophetic gifts. Remain humble and teachable. If you operate in God's grace, in His time, He will make a way for you.

A Prophetic Warning

It's true. God often reveals the devil's plans to His praying and prophetically gifted people. Years ago, while I (Eddie) served on the staff of a local church in Houston, Texas, myself and five other pastors received several warnings from our prophetic intercessors. The warnings concerned sexual temptation, those who submitted them to us, felt that we pastors were about to face. God says every word is to be established by two or three witnesses. (Deuteronomy 19:15b) We had more than enough confirming words to establish this as a legitimate warning.

Prophetic Integrity

So, one day during our weekly pastors' prayer time, we made a commitment to walk in account-ability with each other concerning this issue. We rehearsed our pastoral counseling rules.

1. Any time a male pastor counsels with a woman, he will leave his office door ajar.

2. Never will he do so after hours, when the office staff was gone.

For several weeks we prayed for each other. One night near the end of that period, I had a very vivid dream that clearly indicated the test was over. I shared the dream with the staff the next morning. They concurred with me that this was a word from the Lord and that we had passed the test.

Had it not been for the warnings from our intercessors we pastors might not have been alerted to the enemy's scheme. Not alerted, we might not have been watchful and have taken precautions. Had we not taken precautions, we might have fallen into the enemy's snare. Thank God for the prophetic voices in His body.

Establish a Communication System

Once in a conversation, a friend of ours referenced a sister church that was damaged by poor stewardship and misuse of the prophetic gifts. He said, "If that church had employed some of the safeguards you folks employ, they wouldn't have had the problems they've had with prophetic gifts."

To which we explained, "Had they not have had problems with the prophetic, we would have never established these safeguards!"

Where ministries haven't utilized the revelatory gifts properly, leadership has in large part been "flying blind." We long to see the mature ministry of the revelatory. To achieve this, we must patiently teach our ministry team members spiritual discernment, revelatory responsibility, and accountability. How to recognize and avoid excesses is essential to the well-being of the Body of Christ. The capacity to know right from wrong is available to each of us in whom the Spirit of Truth lives. Notice, *"The spiritual man makes judgments* (proper discernment) *about all things"* (1 Corinthians 2:15).

Communion with God and hearing Him are clearly interrelated. To spend time in His presence sharpens our discernment. As we exercise gifts like prophecy, we grow in discernment. The writer of Hebrews tells us it comes with time and use. *"But solid food is for the mature, who by constant use have trained themselves to distinguish good from evil"* (Hebrews 5:14).

Chapter Fifteen
Public Prophetic Words

We tend to discourage public sharing of prophetic words without prior leadership approval. According to 1 Corinthians 14:29, prophetic words are to be the norm in corporate worship, but don't overlook the guidelines and precautions in that chapter. Prophetic ministry is so immature in many of our churches and ministries today that it is unwise (at least at this time) for it to be exercised publicly without some additional safeguards.

You may wish to encourage anyone with a spontaneous vision, or prophetic message in a church service to clear the word privately with you or a member of your pastoral staff before anyone shares it with the entire congregation.

Prophetic words are sometimes incorrect.

Sometimes the words are correct, but they are simply "out of order."

At other times, *they are the order!*

As prophetically gifted people mature, they can be released more often in public ministry.

Prophetic Integrity

The following newspaper clipping touched our hearts.

ASSOCIATED PRESS: Topeka, KS -- Richard Miller spent three years on a waiting list for a new heart, then missed a chance for a transplant because he couldn't afford to pay his telephone bill and service was cut off.

"The good news was they found me a heart," Miller said Tuesday. "The bad news was I didn't get it 'cause they couldn't contact me."

The heart became available Tuesday morning at the University of Kansas Medical Center in Kansas City.

The 60-year-old Miller suffered three heart attacks that year, then was told he could no longer work. He began receiving Social Security payments of $434 a month. But bills piled up and he could not pay them….

Officials at the medical center called his sister shortly after 9 o'clock a.m. Tuesday and left a message on her answering machine. The hospital called police and asked officers to go to Miller's house.

Miller's sister arrived home later that morning, raced to his house and found a police officer knocking on the door. Miller was asleep. He had missed his chance for a new heart.[13]

Today God's Church, like the lost, needs a "new heart." Spiritual communication is critical to our survival. More than ever, prophetic revelation is needed today to awaken the Church. Are you equipped and released to receive the call? Ask the Father to equip you to hear His voice more clearly, and step out and risk.

NOTES:

1. C. Peter Wagner, John Eckhart chapter, *The New Apostolic Churches* (Ventura, CA: Regal Books, 1998), p. 54.

2. C. Peter Wagner, *Confronting the Powers* (Ventura, CA: Regal Books, 1996), p. 55.

3. Dick Eastman, *The Jericho Hour* (Orlando, FL:, Creation House, 1994), p. 122.

4. John and Paula Sandford, *The Elijah Task* (Tulsa, OK: Victory House, Inc., 1977), pp.154-155.

5. Rev. G.B.F Hallock, *Best Illustrations*, Illus. 702 (New York: Harper and Brothers Publishers; 1935), p. 114.

6. Chuck Pierce & Rebecca Wagner Sytsema, *Possessing Your Inheritance*

(Ventura, CA: Regal Books, 1999), p. 115.

7. Dutch Sheets, *Intercessory Prayer* (Ventura, CA: Regal Books, 1996) pp.225-226.

8. Jennifer LeClaire, *The Danger of Presumptuous Prophets*.

http://www.charismamag.com/blogs/the-plumb-line/20186-the-danger

9. John and Paula Sandford, *The Elijah Task* (Tulsa, OK: Victory House, 1977), p. 55.

10. Eddie and Alice Smith,

http://ministrytodaymag.com/index.php/ministry-today-archives/66-unorganized/16152-picking-up-the-prophetic-pieces#sthash.MxbLlouq.dpuf

11. *Letters*, Charisma Magazine, August 1999, pp. 9-10.

12. C. Peter Wagner, *Pastors & Prophets* (Colorado Springs, CO:

Wagner Publications, 2000). P. 29.

13. Houston Post: 9/16/93

For contact, other books and resources go to:
www.USPrayerCenter.org

www.PrayerBookstore.com

usprayercenter@cs.com

800-569-4825

www.ingramcontent.com/pod-product-compliance
Lightning Source LLC
LaVergne TN
LVHW021501080426
835509LV00018B/2367